For Monika and Marek

THE GARDEN
OF
THE GODS

Plants in Ancient Greece

A History

Magdalena Czajkowska

CONTENTS

O to reach that quiet garden by the Western shore

Where the Daughters of the Evening sing

Under the golden apple tree

Where the god of the dark seas

Has barred the sailor's further passage

Where Atlas guards

The solemn frontiers of the heavens;

Where fountains of ambrosial wine

Flow by Zeus's marriage-couch

And holy Earth

Offers her bounty of delicious fruits

To bless the feast of the immortal gods

Euripides - *Hippolytus*

INTRODUCTION

The ancient Greeks referred to the nebulous mists of prehistory as Chaos. Once it had separated into sky, earth, and sea, the gods fought for sovereignty over them. Out of the titanic struggle there emerged a victor – Zeus – who became the supreme ruler. He divided the spheres of influence among his brothers. To Poseidon he gave the sea, to Hades the underworld, and the sky he kept for himself. The earth with all its vegetation was left to the Olympian gods, named after their residence on Mount Olympus in Northern Greece. It became their garden which they oversaw from above, ensuring it was properly tended by the mortals below, allowing them to use plants for survival, worship, and enjoyment.

Between them the gods presided over all aspects of plant life. Their patronage covered both the natural habitats and cultivated crops. On occasions it extended to the creation of new species through command or transformation. By transforming the mortals into plants the gods conferred on them the gift of immortality, in the sense of abiding in human memory, the plant serving as a living reminder of their life history or their deeds. One way or another, through transformation, dedication, or possession, a plant that came to be associated with a particular deity or hero acquired an additional quality – that of a symbol. From it grew a spectrum, indeed a language, of expression more eloquent than words, which has persisted in art and celebrations of rites of passage to this day.

The symbolic use of plants stretches back to prehistory. Flowers identified by their pollen had already been found in Neanderthal burial sites, placed there perhaps as a symbolic expression of grief, or as a send-off on a journey to the next world. Stories and myths that have accrued to plants have since been commemorated in literature, in stone, on pottery, and on coins.

Alongside the myths and legends of ancient Greece, and fanciful claims of magical powers, ran a course of rational enquiry into the plant kingdom. Among the first to undertake it was the Greek philosopher Theophrastus (400-300 BC) head of the philosophical school, the Lyceum. He decided to take a break from philosophical discussion and set out to observe the verdant world around him. Methodical by nature, and with no precedent to guide him, he listed the flowers as they appeared throughout the seasons. His curiosity led him to enquire also into how plants were used by people, making detailed notes as he went along, what they ate and drank, the perfumes they wore and how they were made up, what went into the composition and choice of wreaths and garlands so popular in his time, which plants healed and which killed. Once collected, he published them in the extant *The History of Plants and Causes of Plants* which was to earn him the title of the Father of Botany (the word derives from the Greek *botanikos* – plant). When he died, he left his private garden to the citizens of Athens.

Among those with a particular interest in the medical properties of plants included the Greek physician Hippocrates (c.500 BC), regarded as the Father of Medicine, and the physician Dioscorides (AD 1) who collected their data in a 'Herbal'. This served as a medical textbook for over fifteen centuries.

The role of plants in the everyday life of the ancient Greeks cannot be overstated. Survival apart, they played an essential part in the performance of social rituals and religious observance, chosen for their association with venerated gods and heroes. This was further stressed by the travel writer of the second century AD, Pausanias, author of *The Guide to Greece*, who carefully noted those species of plants he came across during his travels as he visited the temples and sanctuaries of local deities.

A short glossary of the gods and heroes is provided to accompany this field trip to the ancient Greek world. The plants are listed according to how they were used. Some appear under more than one heading. There are instances where a single herb will flavour food, have medicinal properties, be endowed with 'magic', and even crown the heads of notability or an athlete.

Scientific names are provided in the 'Botanic Names of Plants' for ease of identification. The *exact* identification of some plants mentioned in ancient texts has tested many scholars, botanists, and historians. The aim here is to attach a story taken from the history of ancient Greece to a species familiar in the present day.

FIELD FLOWERS AND THEIR STORIES

The Basket of Europa

While the gods wished for nothing better than to amuse themselves as they looked down on their earthly domain, the mortals set out to make sense of the vegetation around them. The first to embark on a systematic study of the flora was Theophrastus. Having no precedent, he took as his starting point the season of Spring. The fields of Greece in the Spring are unbelievably lovely, covered in a wealth of greenery and a profusion of flowers – a sight that would astonish the visitor who knows Greece only from the summer and autumn months, the parched earth dotted with wisps of dry grass and thistles, where a goat or a donkey might wander in a forlorn search for food.

Theophrastus listed the flowers in order of their appearance. The first, he noted, were the Pink and the Wild Wallflower, popular with the garland makers. Then followed: Pheasant's Eye, Polyanthus, Narcissus, Mountain Anemone, Grape Hyacinth, Violet, Gold Flower, Meadow Anemone, Corn Flag, Squill, and last, the queen of them all – the Rose.

The joy of Spring is reflected in a celebrated myth, perpetuated in stone and coins[1], of a beautiful maiden called Europa, daughter of the legendary king of Tyre. She set out one Spring morning with her companions to pick flowers in a field, holding a basket engraved with scenes from the love story of Zeus and his mistress Io, a family heirloom made by the Olympian goldsmith god, the lame Hephaestus. Yet another of Zeus's amatory exploits was about to take place.

Ignorant of what was to come, Europa and her companions ran out into the field:

When the girls reached the meadows, thick in blossom,
they shared with delight their deep love of the flowers
the fragrant narcissus, the dark hyacinth,
the violet, thyme – for the fields were rich.
Spring filled the air and its blossom the earth.

Moschus, c150 BC. "Europa"[2]

Later that day Europa was abducted by Zeus. Struck by her beauty, he took the form of a docile bull, tossed her on his back and swam to Crete, where he seduced her. According to one version this took place in a willow thicket, as shown on the coins of Gortyna. Theophrastus, however, wrote of a plane tree in Gortyna which does not lose its leaves 'and the story is that under this tree Zeus lay with Europa'.

The Story of the Anemone

According to legend, the Anemones were sent by the wind Anemos to herald the arrival of Spring. Hence their name, translated from the Greek – *anemone* – the Windflower, or Daughter-of-the-Wind.

---

[1] As testified in sculpture (e.g., a metope from temple in Selinus) and coins (e.g., stater from Gortyna c.300 BC depicting Europa sitting in a willow tree)
[2] Moschus – poet c.150 BC, tr. Anthony Holden, Greek Pastoral Poetry, Penguin, 1974, p.183

The red-flowered Anemone was believed to have sprung from the blood of Adonis, the handsome mortal lover of the goddess Aphrodite, wounded while hunting on Mount Lebanon – 'the stony Lebanon where grows his red anemone'[3]. He was gored by a wild boar and bled to death. Aphrodite came too late to save him. As she wept over his body, red Anemones sprung from his blood, white Roses from her tears. The poet Bion, however, thought this was the other way round:

Aphrodite sheds tears as Adonis blood
Drop matches drop; on the ground
they mingle, and bring forth flowers.
From the blood grows the rose
From the tears an anemone.

I weep for Adonis; fair Adonis is dead.
Lament for Adonis – Bion[4]

But then poetic licence might apply here, and the 'Rose' might well have been the red Anemone.

The Latin poet Ovid was moved to describe the appearance of the Anemone:

[Aphrodite] sprinkled Adonis' blood with sweet smelling nectar and, at the touch of the liquid, the blood swelled up ... within an hour, a flower sprang up, the colour of blood... But the enjoyment of this flower is of brief duration: for it is so fragile, its petals so lightly attached, that it quickly falls, shaken from its stem by those same winds that give it its name, Anemone.[5]

The scarlet colour of the Anemone was said to be so alluring it drove virgins to distraction, helped no doubt by the conjured-up vision of the

---

[3] Its scientific name *Adonis annua* bears it out.
[4] Greek pastoral poet c. 100 BC *'Lament for Adonis'* tr. Anthony Holden, Penguin 1974. p.169
[5] Ovid: *Metamorphoses*, tr. Mary M. Innes, Penguin Classics 1977, p.245

handsome Adonis.

The Story of the Bear's Breech (Acanthus)

We have to thank the Bear's Breech, a fairly common plant, for the appearance of Corinthian column in the Greek architecture. Its invention is attributed to an Athenian sculptor Callimachus (late fifth century BC) inspired by the sight of a basket of flowers entwined by the curling leaves of the Bear's Breech he saw placed on a tomb of a young girl. He reproduced it in stone on a capital intended for a temple column, and a new, flamboyant style was born. The earliest known Corinthian capital is to be found in the temple of Apollo at Bassae. Little remains there, but later examples abound. The Corinthian style flourished up to, and especially during Roman times, and has been reproduced ever since.

This 'smiling Acanthus' became the symbol of the love of fine arts, widely applied in painting and pottery.

The Story of the Corn Flag

Once upon a time a Cyclops whose name was Polyphemus fell in love with a nymph called Galatea. (Cyclops were giant shepherds with a single eye across the forehead.) In the words of a poet,[6] 'he loved her not with apples, with roses, or locks of hair, but with headlong passion'. Galatea, however, was in love with a young shepherd called Acis, and not at all interested in Polyphemus. So, the heartbroken Polyphemus would sit on the cliffs overlooking the sea to watch Galatea take her daily swim and tried to console himself by making up songs about his unrequited love. One day, as he took his customary walk to the seashore, he saw Galatea and Acis embracing each other. Seized with terrible rage, he hurled a rock at Acis, crushing him to death. His blood, trickling from

---

[6] Theocritus *The Cyclops*, tr. Anthony Holden, p.88

under the rock, formed a stream which began to flow at the feet of the sobbing Galatea. From the clefts in the rock sprang the Corn Flags.

The Story of the Honesty

The Honesty was known as 'the flower of the cow', or 'the flower of Io'. Io was the daughter of Inachus, first king of Argos, with whom Zeus fell in love. To hide her from his jealous wife Hera, Zeus changed Io into a cow. To provide suitable nourishment for her he caused the Honesty to spring up.

Hera, however, was not easily deceived, and ordered Argus, a hundred-eyed monster that never slept, to watch Io. When Zeus realised what was going on, he called on the god Hermes to get rid of the monster. Hermes obliged by lulling Argus to sleep with his music, then killed him. Undaunted, Hera set Argus's eyes into the tail of a peacock, then sent a gadfly to torment Io. The gadfly drove the frenzied Io from place to place, until she found rest on the banks of the Nile. Once back in human form, Io bore Zeus a son who later became a king of Egypt. The Ionian Sea is named after her, as is the Bosphorus – literally 'the cow's ford'.

The Story of the Larkspur

The Larkspur's former scientific name was *Delphinium ajacis,* based on the resemblance of its bud form to a dolphin (Greek *delphis*). 'Ajacis' refers to the story of its origin which took place at the time of the death of Ajax, hero of Troy.

Ajax, son of Telamon, king of Salamis, sailed for Troy with twelve ships. His fame for bravery in battle was second only to that of Achilles. When the Trojan hero Hector was killed by Achilles, both Ajax and Odysseus claimed Hector's arms. Odysseus won the claim which enraged Ajax to the point of momentarily losing his mind. In a fit he slaughtered all the sheep of the army, mistaking them for the enemy. On recovering his senses, confronted with the carnage he had wrought, overcome by shame and remorse, he committed suicide by falling on a sword stuck into the ground. Where he fell Larkspurs sprang up, and, at the same time, all over his native Salamis. Larkspurs have markings on their petals which the Greeks identified with the letters 'AI', interpreted as exclamations of grief: Ai, Ai, woe, woe.

This is the flower alluded to in one of Virgil's Eclogues. "Question: 'Say, in what country do flowers grow with the name of kings written upon them? Answer: Delphinium, as it is said to have sprung from the blood of Ajax who, when defeated by Ulysses, ended his own life'".

On the other hand, Pausanias described the flower that appeared in Salamis at the time of Ajax's death as white with a tinge of pink, smaller than a lily, but marked with the 'letters' like that of the Hyacinth. The orchid *Orchis quadripunctato* has been suggested by scholars as a possible alternative to this flower of lamentation.[7]

The Story of the Hyacinth

The sweet-scented Hyacinth is the parent of our cultivated Hyacinth. Its petals have markings similar to the Larkspur's.

> *The violet is dark*
> *Dark the lettered hyacinth*
> *Yet all these flowers*
> *Are counted the first…*
>
> *Theocritus: The Idylls – The Reapers*[8]

---

[7] Pausanias 'Guide to Greece' vol. I, pub. Penguin 1978, tr. Peter Levi, p.100
[8] tr. Anthony Holden, Greek Pastoral Poetry p.36

The origin of the Hyacinth is traced to the god Apollo who fell in love with a beautiful Spartan prince called Hyacinthus, the first god, it is claimed, to fall in love with one of the same sex (Zeus must have carried off the cup-bearer Ganymedes later). Hyacinthus also caught the fancy of Zephyrus, the West Wind, who became obsessively jealous of him. One day, when Apollo and Hyacinthus were having a game of quoits, Zephyrus caught the quoit in mid-air and dashed it against the youth's head, killing him instantly. From his blood sprang the Hyacinth (though some say it was a gladiolus)[9]. The markings on the flower petals, 'inscribed with the syllable of lament', recall either sorrow or the initials of the Greek version of the youth's name, AI.

A festival called Hyacinthia was celebrated in Amyclae (near Sparta), in honour of Hyacinthus where he was worshipped as a hero. It lasted three days, during which youths played various musical instruments and chanted songs in honour of Apollo, followed by dancing and more singing. There were also chariot races for girls, beautifully dressed in richly decorated chariots. The festivities ended with offerings on the altar of Apollo.

Hyacinthus' acclaimed beauty made the phrase 'hyacinthine locks' very popular with artists and poets.

The Story of the Narcissus

The Narcissus flower made its appearance at the untimely death of a beautiful youth from Boeotia called Narcissus. He was so exceptionally handsome that those who met him could not help but fall in love with him, none more so than a nymph called Echo. He, however, was as indifferent to her as to all his suitors. To one of his more persistent suitors he even sent a sword, indicating spurned love. On receiving it the

---

[9] William T. Stearn 'Stearn's Dictionary of Plant Names for Gardeners' pub. Cassell 2004, p.170

poor man killed himself. As he lay dying, he invoked Aphrodite, the goddess of love, to avenge him. She heard his prayer and decided to punish Narcissus with a love that could never be consummated.

Her chance came when Narcissus went hunting in the mountains, followed by the lovelorn nymph Echo who could only use her voice by repeating the voice of others, a punishment meted out by Hera when she discovered Echo was sent by Zeus to divert her with long stories while he went off on his amatory pursuits. Unable to express her love (as Narcissus never uttered any words of endearment), she could only follow him mutely at a discreet distance.

While Narcissus was chasing a deer, he stopped by a pool of clear, undisturbed water. The surface of the water clearly reflected his face as he kneeled down to drink. Seeing himself for the first time, he was amazed by his own beauty. He lay for hours spellbound, gazing at his reflected image, trying in vain to embrace it. Finally he drowned, mourned by the silent Echo, though some say he stabbed himself, unable to accept the futility of his passion. From the spot where he died beautiful, scented flowers sprang up bearing his name, the yellow cups specially formed to contain his (and presumably Echo's) tears.

'Nonsense,' wrote Pausanias. 'The boy was old enough to tell the difference between a human being and a reflection. Narcissus was in love with his sister, and he imagined it was *her* reflection he was looking at. Anyway, the flower appeared before his time, created by Hades to lure Persephone to his underworld kingdom.'[10]

The flower is indeed sacred to Hades, the god of the underworld, who fell in love with a maiden called Persephone, daughter of the goddess Demeter. Not inclined to protracted courtship, he sent up a beautiful Narcissus when she was picking flowers in a meadow, in order to lure her to a place where he could abduct her. As Persephone bent down to

---

[10] Pausanias 'Guide to Greece' vol. I, pub. Penguin 1978, tr. Peter Levi, p.376-377

pick it, the earth opened at her feet, up sprang Hades, in a magnificent chariot drawn by black horses, swept her up and rushed back to his underground kingdom. The earth closed behind them, leaving no trace of the incident. Thus the Narcissus became associated with the underworld. A species (*N. papyraceus*) apparently crowned its dreadful inhabitants, the Furies or Eumenides lurking there.

For the mortals it was a source of the *narcotic* drug. It continues to be regarded as a flower of deceit and as a symbol of self-esteem and fatuity, borne out by the legend of the youth who fell in love with himself (Pausanias's comments notwithstanding).

The Story of the Squill

The imposing inflorescence of the Squill, rising at least three feet above the ground, brings welcome relief to an arid summer landscape. The Squill was dedicated to the god Pan whose cult was widespread in Arcadia. His name means 'all', because his half-man half-goat appearance amused *all* the gods. The mortals, on the other hand, tended to be seized with fright at his sudden appearance which would throw them into a 'panic' (the root of the word traced to the naughty god who delighted in causing irrational terror).

Pan was a fertility god, patron of woods and pastures, the deity of shepherds and protector of flocks and herds, invoked to make goats and ewes fecund. If prayers were not answered his statues were beaten with Squills. 'Do this, dear Pan', went a prayer, 'and may the Arcadian boys never more chastise you with their squills when they're underfed ...'[11] This referred to the young musicians of Arcadia, who needed full stomachs to sing well, and blamed Pan for insufficient food.

Sea Squills and Fig branches were used to whip two men who ran through the streets of Athens during the festivities in honour of Artemis

---

[11] Theocritus: The Idylls VII, The Harvest Feast tr. Anthony Holden p.77

in April (Munychia) to drive out defilement from the city.[12]

Squill bulbs were hung in houses in the New Year fertility rites. Planted before the entrance to the door of a house, they warded off defilement and any mischief that might threaten, according to Theophrastus.

The bulb roasted and dried was used as a remedy for stomach and kidney disorders. Its diuretic and purgative properties were especially effective in combating bile. When somebody had worked up a truly bad temper, it was wise to procure Squills: 'Is someone getting wild? Dig up some witch's grave and get him squills', says a character in Theocritus's "The Idylls". [13]

The bulb was notably 'tenacious of life' wrote Theophrastus, a fact borne out on seeing the Squill flower in a parched ground, where no rain fell for several weeks. It also kept fresh any food stored in it, such as edible stalks, for a long time.

The Fennel of Prometheus

The Titan[14] Prometheus was the acknowledged champion and protector of the mortals who took it upon himself to intercede with Zeus on their behalf. When Zeus demanded the best part of animals to be sacrificed to him, Prometheus decided to intervene. He killed a bull, separated the bones from the meat and wrapped them in glistening fat. The meat he hid in an unappetizing stomach lining, then invited Zeus to choose his sacrificial due. Unaware of the deception, Zeus carelessly pointed to the rich pieces of fat. On discovering the mistake, yet unable to go back on his word, he flew into a rage and decreed that though men can keep the

---

[12] Robert Flacelière, 'Daily Life in Greece at the time of Pericles' pub. Phoenix 2002, tr. Robert Green, p.203
[13] Theocritus: The Idylls: The Goatherd versus the Shepherd, tr. Anthony Holden, Greek Pastoral Poetry, p.70
[14] Titans – pre-Olympian gods or demi-gods

meat, they will have to eat it raw. So wrote the poet Hesiod[15], who traced the ancestry of the first races of men to an ash tree, '... Zeus who knows the imperishable counsels ... would not give the force of weariless fire [to the ash-people]' [16].

Prometheus stepped in again. He took a glowing ember from the fire burning in the gods' residence and hid it in the hollow stalk of a fennel. 'The strong man of Iapetos [i.e., Prometheus] outwitted him [Zeus] and stole the far-seen glory of the weariless fire, hiding it in the hollow fennel stalk'[17]. Prometheus handed it to a man called Phoronus, instructing him in the use of fire.[18]

For this challenge to the authority of the ruler of gods and men, Prometheus was cruelly punished. He was chained to a lonely rock in the Caucasus where an eagle pecked at his liver all day. It healed during the night, only to be pecked by the eagle the following day. After thousands of years of this torture, Prometheus was finally released by the hero Heracles.

The story of Prometheus inspired his recipients with an indomitable spirit – to challenge the gods and bow to no one. They paid homage to the gods, of course, and bowed to the inevitability of fate, yet abhorred tyranny and absolute rule, evolving a democratic form of government unique for its time. Their belief in the freedom of the individual led them to enquire and question all around them. As Socrates[19] famously said: 'Life without enquiry is not worth living', echoed by Euripides[20]: 'Happy is he who has knowledge that comes from inquiry'.

---

[15] Hesiod, poet from Boeotia c. 700 BC – *Theogony*
[16] Hesiod – *Theogony, The Creation of Woman*, tr. Richmond Lattimore, Greek Literature in Translation, p.58
[17] Hesiod, ibid.
[18] Though the Argives believed it was Phoronus who discovered the use of fire, and worshipped him as a hero. In the temple in the city of Argos there was a perpetual fire burning, called the fire of Phoronus
[19] Socrates, philosopher 469-399 BC
[20] Euripides: *The Study of Nature'* tr. C. M. Bowra, Greek Literature in Translation, Penguin, p.149

The Greeks were not prepared even to perform gestures of submission, neither in prayer (they did not kneel) nor making obeisance as required by the court etiquette. The historian Herodotus recounts a story of two Spartans forcefully ordered to prostrate themselves in the presence of a Persian king. They refused, saying: 'They would never do any such thing, even were their heads thrust down to the ground, for it was not their custom to worship men'.[21]

The Giant Fennel associated with Prometheus is but a humble reminder of that spirit.

The sturdy stalks of the fennel topped with Pinecones, entwined with Ivy, were used as staffs or *thyrsii* by the female companions of Dionysus, the Maenads. 'One woman struck her *thyrsus* against a rock ... Another drove her fennel into the ground, and where it struck the earth /at the touch of god, a spring of wine poured out"[22].

Fennel was considered to be a plant of spiritual (and bodily) regeneration. It was believed serpents acquired their periodic regeneration (in shedding their skin) by eating its leaves. Medicinally it was considered good for 'clearing the sight'.

ADDITIONAL NOTES

Coltsfoot

'Coltsfoot is an Arcadian herb, all the foals run mad for it, all the mares around the hills ...'[23] wrote the Greek pastoral poet Theocritus.

---

[21] Herodotus, *'Histories, Book VII'*, tr. George Rawlinson, Wordsworth Classics 1996, p.560

[22] Euripides, *The Bacchae*, tr. William Arrowsmith, Greek Literature in Translation, Penguin, p.156

[23] Theocritus, *The Idylls, The Sorceress*, tr. Anthony Holden, p.53

WREATHS

A Greek simply did not feel fully dressed it seems, unless they were wearing a wreath. Wreaths and chaplets were worn on any and every possible occasion – ceremonial, private functions, or indeed for no particular reason. 'I would have come to see you,' says a young man to a girl, 'bringing you apples, with a wreath tied with purple band round my brow ...'[24]

Wreaths were sold in markets, woven by women who made them up to customers' instructions:

> *Woman:*   *You want some garlands, maybe; if you do*
> *Shall they be myrtles, thyme, or Flowers-all-through?*
> *Purchaser:* *We want those myrtles you've got there.*
> *You can keep the others.*
> Euboulos (tr. Edmonds)[25]

One might also turn to a poet:

[24] Theocritus, *The Idylls, The Sorceress*
[25] From: *Garden Lore of Ancient Athens*, pub. American School of Classical Studies at Athens, Princeton, New Jersey 1963, quoting a play

I will weave the violet white,
Mid the myrtle weave the light
Jonquill, and therewith I will
Weave the laughing daffodil.
Then the saffron sweet of smell,
Weave I will, and weave as well
Purple iris, and with those
Interweave the true-love rose,
So, on the brow where clusters fair,
Heliodora's fragrant hair,
This my coronal will fling
Every flower of the Spring.

Meleager, *Heliodora's Wreath*, tr. R. A. Furness[26]

Wreaths and garlands were not only worn, but also given as presents, much as bouquets of flowers nowadays. 'You will make me tear this garland to pieces, Amaryllis, my love,' says a disgruntled lover. 'This crown I made for you of ivy, of rosebuds and sweet celery'.[27]

According to Theophrastus, the most popular wreath flowers were: Rose, Anemone, Violets, Carnations, Lily, Parsley, Greenbrier (Smilax), Gold Flower (very popular), and the fruits of Cotoneaster. Those that went into the composition of a wreath were not chosen haphazardly, though obviously subject to seasonal availability. A whole range of symbolism was brought into force in order to convey the mood of the wearer or the intentions of the giver.

Wreaths had not only to be symbolically eloquent; but also in good taste. They reflected on the wearer, and could provoke a disdainful remark, such as: 'some people (who should know better) would join

---

[26] Meleager, poet and philosopher c.100 BC
[27] Theocritus, *The Idylls: The Serenade*, tr. Anthony Holden, Greek Pastoral Poetry p.58

garlic and roses to make a wreath!'[28]

Another factor governing the composition of wreaths, particularly if worn to a banquet, was their supposed remedial qualities. Two distinguished Greek physicians, Mnestheus and Callimachus, even compiled books on the properties of wreaths. Some plants, such as Stock or Marjoram, were considered capable of stupefying or oppressing the brain. Some did the opposite – they alleviated headaches and even counteracted the effects of wine (Myrtle was supposed to be very good for that).

Invited to a formal banquet in Athens, attended, as was customary, only by men (though dancing and flute-girls provided after-dinner entertainment), the guests prepared themselves by going to perfumers, barbers, and garlanders. Plato wrote of an incident at a dinner at which Socrates was present, when a very drunk Alcibiades[29] turned up 'wearing a thick-plaited wreath of ivy and violets, all hung up with ribands'[30].

The main meal over, water was brought in for the guests to wash their hands, followed by more perfumes and garlands. Libations and a hymn to Dionysus followed. After that, wine mixed with water flowed, the assembled company recited poetry, sang songs, played riddles and other games, entertained by slave girls playing the lyre (*kithara*). The evening ended with an unsteady walk back home:

Boy, hold my wreath for me
The night is black
The path is long
And I am completely and beautifully drunk.

The Determined Serenader – Anon.[31]

---

[28] Attributed to Atheneus
[29] Alcibiades – Athenian politician and general
[30] Plato's *Symposium* quoted by Robert Flaciere, *Daily life in Greece in the time of Pericles*, p.177
[31] Homer, *The Iliad* tr. Dudley Fitts, *Greek Literature in Translation*, Penguin 1973, p.354

Most famously wreaths were presented to the winners of athletic games. At the Olympic Games, the winner received a wreath of Wild Olive, chosen for its association with the original founder of the games, the supreme hero Heracles, who brought a Wild Olive tree from the land of the Hyperboreans, 'men who lived beyond the home of the North wind'. The winner's wreath was woven from the sacred Wild Olive tree called the Crown Olive, growing in the Olympic precincts. To win the Olympic Olive wreath was the ultimate goal of every athlete.

The famous gold and ivory statue of Zeus presiding at Olympia was described by Pausanias: 'There was a wreath of twigs and leaves of olive on his head and his cloak was inlaid with animals and flowering lilies.'[32] A tiny statue of Victory perched on his right hand was also crowned with a wreath. The image of Zeus's statue was stamped on the coins of Olympia. A silver coin from Elis (under whose auspices the Olympic Games were celebrated) bore Zeus's head wearing a Wild Olive wreath.

In the Nemean Games a wreath of Wild Celery (or Parsley) was the victor's award. 'He was *green* with Korinthian parsley'[33] wrote the poet Pindar in praise Timarsachos, winner in the boys' wrestling competition.

In the Pythian Games at Delphi, a wreath of Bay leaves (i.e., Laurel) was the ultimate award, the laurel being sacred to Apollo, whose oracle presided in Delphi.

The victor of Isthmian Games received a wreath of the evergreen Pine.

In addition to a wreath, a Palm branch was given to the winner to be carried in the right hand, a tradition traced to the hero Theseus, who held the games at Apollo's shrine in Delphi and was crowned with branches of the Palm growing there.

In competitions of music, drama, and poetry, the winners were awarded wreaths of Ivy.

---

[32] Pausanias, *Guide to Greece* vol. II, p.227
[33] Pindar, *Odes, Nemean IV, XI*, tr. C. M. Bowra, *The Odes of Pindar* pub. Penguin 1985, p.115

Ivy wreaths feature on the coins of the city of Philious (N.E. Peloponnese) – it is not clear whether in deference to Dionysus or to Hebe, the goddess of youth.

The magistrates of the city of Athens wore wreaths of Myrtle sacred to Aphrodite as their symbol of office, signifying bloodless victory. In Athens, during an assembly debate, the citizen who took the floor had a Myrtle wreath placed on his head to confer his privileged status.[34]

Wreaths were worn on the days of the rites of passage. In wedding ceremonies, the bride and groom wore garlands of Laurel and Olive, the father of the bride wore one of Myrtle, while the mother held a torch. Myrtle wreaths were also much in evidence in funeral rites.

Distinguished citizens were presented with golden wreaths of Oak, sacred to the supreme god Zeus. Those wreaths were held in great esteem, so much so that replicas made of thinner gold leaf were placed on their tombs.

At religious festivals, garlands were hung on the city gates. On altars decorated with flowers, wreaths were offered to the statue of the deity in whose honour the ceremonies were being celebrated. Everyone assembled wore a wreath – the priests of the divinity, the participants walking in the procession, the sacrificial victims. In the famous case of Iphigenia, sacrificed by her father Agamemnon for a fair wind to Troy, the girl went to her death wearing a wreath. Animals had garlands put round their necks before being sacrificed, that is slaughtered on the altar of a deity. A delightful poem describes a bull about to be sacrificed at one such ceremony:

Thus the gay victim with fresh garlands crowned
Pleased with the sacred pipe's enlivening sound,
Through gazing crowds in solemn state proceeds
And dressed in final pomp, magnificently bleeds.

---

[34] Robert Flacelière, *Daily Life in Greece in the time of Pericles*, pub. Phoenix 2002, tr. Robert Green, p.36

ADDITIONAL NOTES

Dill

This common culinary plant, the Feathery Dill, was very popular with the garland and wreath makers.

> *I'll crown myself with dill*
> *With roses and with snowdrops …'*
>> Song of a goatherd in Theocritus's poem *The Harvest Feast*.

The Story of the Lotus

There was once a young girl who fell in love with Heracles. He, however, remained indifferent to her attentions. She died of unrequited love and was transformed into a Lotus flower.

The Lotus supposedly grew best in Helicon, the dwelling place of the Muses. Through association with those divine inhabitants, it became the symbol of eloquence.

This popular garland flower was mentioned in connection with the marriage of Menelaus king of Sparta and Helen. It also found its way into the nuptial couch of Zeus and Hera:

> *Glad earth perceives, and from her Bosom pours*
> *Unbidden herbs, and voluntary Flow'rs*
> *Thick new-born Vi'lets a soft Carpet spread*
> *And clust'ring Lotos swell'd the rising Bed*
> *And sudden Hyacinths the Turf bestrow*
> *And flamy Crocus made the Mountains glow.*[35]

---

[35] Homer, *The Iliad, Book XIV*, tr. Alexander Pope (1718), *The Oxford Book of Classical Verse* p.22-23

Ivy

The Ivy, firmly associated with Dionysus, principally worshipped as the god of wine, was widely used in the composition of wreaths. The Ivy was also symbolic of love and friendship, because it never leaves its host and grows in close union with it.

SCENTS

The word 'perfume' is derived from the Latin *per fumum* (through smoke), a reference to the prayers offered by priests to the gods through clouds of scented smoke arising from incense bowls or swinging censers. From fragrance burnt it was but a short step for the scents to be worn, to make the priests who served the gods more presentable and pleasing to them. The Egyptian priests anointed themselves ritually with a perfume 'Cyphi' as part of their religious observance. It was mentioned by Dioscorides. '"Cyphi" is the composition of perfume, welcome to ye gods, the priests of Egypt doe use it'.

The habit of wearing perfumes spread from the priests to everybody, and soon fortunes were spent, and made, on them. From early history, caravans of merchants set out to beyond the ends of the then known world to bring back fragrant gums and resins. One can picture those caravans, small and vulnerable in the vastness of the desert, no compasses or maps. Information about what lay ahead was obtained from hearsay and experience of the survivors. Sand squeaking under the splayed feet of camels, men wrapped in garments with only their eyes visible – sharp and wary, always on the lookout for marauding tribesmen, robbers, wild animals. Life was finely poised on the edge of a crude weapon. Many would meet their end on the way, their bleached bones tossed by the wind on endless sands. Some did come through, having bribed their way by levies and gifts. All for what? For perfume ingredients that had to be 'just right'. Not any handy, fragrant herb nature thoughtfully provided on the doorstep, perfumes had to be special – alluring, enchanting, exotic, mysterious, captivating, the stuff of dreams. If it so happened, as it did, that they cost a fortune, well then, a fortune had to be spent. Relating the stories on how gums and spices were collected and brought to the Mediterranean shores, the Roman writer Pliny commented: 'So here is one more trade route that exists chiefly because women follow fashion'.

Once the fashion of wearing perfume had caught on, it never abated, not then, not now. It included everybody, from the Olympian goddesses to simple country girls. The goddess Hera 'smoothed herself, and this her scented oil unstoppered in the bronze-floored household of Zeus, cast fragrance over earth and heaven'[36]. At the opposite end of the scale, country girls made do with pomanders of Rose petals and crushed herbs.

Possibly the earliest reference to a perfume was found inscribed on an Egyptian tomb, dating back to 3,000-3,500 BC, although the first liquid perfume made from fragrant powders mixed with oil is attributed to the Greeks. Perfumes were made from flowers, seeds, fruits soaked in oil and water, sometimes heated, strained through a cloth or from powdered resins dissolved in oils. Flower-scented oils were used to preserve the ivory on statues.

The composition of a perfume was critical, and the skill of the makers of perfumes was a much-valued skill. Mycenean kings had perfume makers in their retinue, Persian kings never went anywhere without them. Excavations of the Minoan palace of Zakros[37] revealed workshops where utensils for preparations of aromatic substances were found, together with lumps of resins for making incense.

---

[36] Homer, *The Iliad* Book 14, tr. Robert Fitzgerald, pub. OUP, p.244
[37] Crete, built around 1,700-1,450 BC

In classical Athens perfumes could be obtained from shops called '*Unguentarii*', competing in popularity with the stalls of the garland-makers. Theophrastus literally sniffed his way around them, recording his findings in the chapter 'Concerning odours'[38]. He talked to the perfumers, asked their opinion on popularity, colour, the lasting quality of perfumes, and the kind of containers they were kept in. Perfumes had to be kept in special containers, he was told. Coolness and closeness of texture was required for this purpose. Best for these volatile substances easily destroyed by heat were vessels of lead or phials of alabaster. The slim little bottles containing perfumes were called *alabastrums,* the small oil jugs *aryballos.* Some had lovely shapes and intricate designs. One preserved for us from the sixth century BC was made in the form of a cluster of shells with an inscription round its lip 'handsome youth indeed'.

The most frequently used oil in perfumery was derived either from the Egyptian or Syrian Balanos followed by the purified native Olive oil or Almond oil. The order in which the ingredients were added to the oil was important, the last one imparting the strongest smell.

Of the home-grown ingredients most commonly used were:

Herbs – Thyme, Rosemary, Lavender, Mint, Sage. Particular in demand were the fragrant herbs of Crete – the Oregano and the Verbena.

Fruit – Myrtle, Bay, Quince

Flowers – most esteemed – the Rose, closely followed by the Lily, Jasmine, Violet. For the Violet-smelling perfumes the root of the Florentine Iris, source of the *orris* which gives off a smell of Violets when powdered. No list of popular perfumes in antiquity would be complete without the scented flowers of Henna (cultivated to this day) and the Saffron.

Theophrastus also listed the plants provided by the perfume makers: Cassia, Cinnamon, Cardamom, Spikenard, Balsam of Mecca, Storax,

---

[38] Theophrastus, *The History of Plants*

Iris, 'Nartekostos', All-heal, Saffron Crocus, Myrrh, 'Kypeiron', Ginger Grass, Sweet Flag, Sweet Marjoram, 'Lotos', Dill. The Iris perfume, he was told, had the smallest number of ingredients. The sacred perfume of the Egyptian priests, the 'Cyphi[39]', of which Queen Cleopatra was reputedly particularly fond, had no fewer than sixteen ingredients. It contained, among others, Myrrh, Saffron, Juniper, Cypress, as well as other resins mixed with wine. The resulting perfume 'will lull to sleep, allay anxieties and brighten dreams. It is made of things that delight in the night'[40].

For women the best perfumes were Myrrh oil, 'Megaleion', Sweet Marjoram, Spikenard, and the Egyptian perfumes. 'That's what women require.' As for men their favoured choice was the light '*kypros*' derived from the flowers of Henna.

The popular 'Megaleion' was made up of burnt resin, oil of Balanos[41] mixed with Cassia, Cinnamon, Myrrh, and a red dye. Into the 'Sweet Marjoram' perfume, Theophrastus tells us, went all kinds of spices and plants with the exception of the Sweet Marjoram itself! The name is misleading he concludes.

On the whole perfumes were coloured, mostly red. For this purpose, Alkanet was used, or a substance called khroma extracted from the root of a plant native to Syria. Only a few perfumes were acceptable colourless.

Perfumes lasted a varying length of time. On the whole compound perfumes were considered to last longer. Myrrh oil reputedly kept for any length of time, whereas perfumes made from flowers would keep from two months to a year. A perfumer told Theophrastus he had kept an Egyptian perfume for eight years and an Iris one for twenty years, and both still retained their freshness.

---

[39] Dioscorides: "Cyphi is the composition of perfume, welcome to ye gods, the priests of Egypt doe use it".
[40] Plutarch: *Opera moralia* 80, Vol.5, Loeb Classical Library 1936
[41] *Balanites aegyptiaca*

The use of perfumes in classical Athens was lavish. As one Athenian put it: 'The shoppers all bathed, babble before it is bright daylight in the wreath market, while others gabble at perfume booths over mint and larkspur'. The same could not be said of the austere Spartans who expelled the perfume makers ostensibly for wasting oil and considered putting scent on the body as effeminate.

After a bath, it was customary to first rub oneself with oil before applying perfumes. Different scents were used for different parts of the body. The sweetest scent reputedly came from the wrist. Mint was recommended for armpits, palm oil for the chest, Marjoram for hair and eyebrows, crushed Thyme for neck and knees. By and large, however, everyone followed individual fancy, and wore at least half a dozen different scents at any one time. No wonder it earned a special mention in the works of Hippocrates on the subject of the dress and behaviour of physicians. 'Physicians', he wrote, 'are required to be clean in person, well dressed and anointed with sweet-smelling unguents that arouse no suspicion!'

Bathed, perfumed, and garlanded, an Athenian would make his way in the cool of an evening to a banquet, to end the day in this pleasant manner. After a meal, which was set on little tables before the guests lying on couches, water was brought in to wash their hands, followed by perfumes to be applied on top of those already worn. On occasion doves were released, their wings drenched in scented oil, spreading fragrance around the banqueting chamber where stood tall incense burners also releasing scent.

Perfumes had medicinal uses. The Rose perfume, for instance, was supposed to alleviate earache, probably thanks also to the large amount of salt and oil it contained. The Myrrh and the Cassia had 'warming' properties considered good for catarrhs. On the other hand, the Spikenard, the 'Megaleion', and the cheap varieties were thought to cause headaches.

Spice and herbs powders were sprinkled on bedding and placed in chests and coffers where clothes were kept to discourage moths and other insects. Odysseus, for instance, kept his clothes in scented coffers. The Citron which has a long-lasting fragrance, was recommended as an excellent insect repellent (and not as fruit to be eaten).

Scented oils anointed the dead. Aphrodite, for instance, lamenting the death of her lover Adonis cried:

Now Adonis is dead. Anoint him
With Syrian perfumes, with oils ...

Bion - Lament for Adonis

Small flasks of perfumed oil, usually containing the 'Orris' obtained from the root of the Iris, were placed in graves with the deceased. To obtain the 'Orris', the most common fixative used in perfumes to preserve and enrich their fragrance, the rhizomes harvested after flowering were dried, ground and stored for two years. On its own it smells of Violets.

'Orris' was also used in cosmetics. Grated, soaked in water, then rubbed on the cheeks reputedly accompanied by a tingling sensation, imparted a rosy complexion.

STORIES OF THE FLOWERS USED IN PERFUMES

Iris

This flower belongs to its namesake, the goddess Iris, 'she who runs upon the wind'[42]. She appears in the Greek mythology as messenger of the gods, particularly of Hera, the goddess of women and marriage. Iris led the dead souls of women (Hermes the men) to the underworld. She is

---

[42] Homer *The Iliad* Book I, 799, p.40

also the personification of the rainbow which links the earth with the sky, hence, by association, the Olympians gods with the mortals. The Iris flower stood also for rejected love and, according to some sources, for eloquence and power.

Rose

The Rose, the 'queen of lovers' hopes, the sweet persuasive rose', was the principal flower of Aphrodite, the goddess of love and beauty, whose enchantments residing in her magic girdle 'made the sanest men into fools' if poets are to be believed. Aphrodite 'ever ... crowns her hair with a fragrant wreath of roses'[43]. Her attendants, the Graces, usually carried Roses, and her son Eros, whose arrows struck men and gods alike by making them fall rashly in love, was also crowned with Roses.

> *"The Rose is the honour of beauty of Floures,*
> *The Rose is the care and love of the Spring:*
> *The Rose is the pleasure of th'heavenly Pow'rs.*
> *The Boy of Faire Venus[44], Cythera's[45]Darling,*
> *Doth wrap his head round with garlands of Roses,*
> *When to the dances of the Graces he goes."*
>
> (Gerard quoting the Greek poet Anacreon[46])

According to legend, Roses turned red when Aphrodite trod on a bush of white Roses as she ran to her dying lover, Adonis, and dripped blood on them. They were also stained red by Eros who, while leading a dance on the Olympus, stumbled and spilled a bowl of nectar. The nectar happened to fall on a Rose bush, changing its colour.

---

[43] Euripides –Athenian tragic poet fifth century BC "Athens" tr. C. M. Bowra, *Greek Poetry in Translation* p.150

[44] Roman name for the Greek Aphrodite

[45] Another name for Aphrodite – she first stepped ashore on the island of Cythera

[46] Anacreon, Greek poet c.570 BC

Once Eros gave a Rose to Harpocrates, the god of silence, not to betray Aphrodite's love affairs. Since then, it became the symbol of secrecy. Others trace the source of this symbolism to a secret meeting held between the Greeks and the Persian king Xerxes held in a Rose bower near a temple of Athena. Hence at banquets, a Rose suspended over the tables reminded the assembled guests not to divulge whatever was being said. To say *sub rosa* ('under the rose') meant to be sworn to secrecy. Roses were subsequently painted on ceilings. A plaster Rose on a ceiling is a common ornament to this day, although its symbolism is probably forgotten.

Treasured for its scent as well as for its appearance, the Rose had admirers everywhere, drawn by its quality of never-failing wonder that goes under the inadequate name of beauty. When poets wrote: 'the rose has a scent surpassing all others', they spoke for everybody. The pastoral poet Theocritus confirmed it in his *Idylls*.[47] 'Anemones and thorns may never match the rose; the dog rose in the shadow of the wall.'

While poets sang praises, Theophrastus decided to look into the cultivated species popular in his time – the Damask and the Hundred-Petalled Rose. The latter is a misnomer, he pointed out. Meticulous as ever, he proceeded to count them and found their number varied. Most flowers had five petals, some had twelve, others twenty or more, and some were indeed hundred-petalled. He also noted variations in roughness, colour, and sweetness of the scent. The flowers had to be gathered between dawn and sunrise when their fragrance was at its the strongest. Those with the strongest scent came from Cyrene (N. Africa) and from Macedonia. It was one of the most popular perfumes and the main component of the precious fragrant oil – the attar or *otto of Roses*.

The Rose was the most popular of all the garden flowers. They grew in the celebrated gardens of the legendary King Midas (whose touch

---

[47] Theocritus – *The Idylls V – The Goatherd versus the Shepherd, Greek Pastoral Poetry* p.68

turned everything into gold) who counted them as one of his not inconsiderable treasures. The satyr Silenus, tutor to the wine god Dionysus, strayed into one of his gardens to sleep off a hangover after a particularly heavy drinking bout. His presence was discovered by the gardeners who brought him to the king's presence. Silenus was made to entertain the king with funny stories for five days and nights (hangover notwithstanding) before being allowed to leave.

One of the best-known Greek gardens worthy of the name (the Greeks were not great gardeners, gardens being mainly intended for edible produce) was established by the philosopher Epicurus, who purchased a plot in Athens reputedly to satisfy his desire for a fresh Rose every day. His school of philosophy came to be known as 'The Garden', and his pupils were referred to as 'Those from the Garden'. Epicurus spent the remainder of his days there, surrounded by his pupils, friends, and, of course, Roses.

The city famous for its Roses was Posidonia (Paestum) in Magna Grecia founded by the Greeks in the sixth century BC Its emblem was a siren holding a Rose. The Roses growing there blossomed twice a year, thanks to the particular quality of the soil. In time, the city lost its soil through the gradual silting of the river, and with it the Roses and its wealth.

Roses flourished also on the island of Rhodes, named after the nymph Rhode ('Rosy'), whose island it was. A Rose, either full blown or in bud, was struck on the coins of the island, (disputed by some scholars who identify it as a pomegranate flower).

The essential oil or attar was derived chiefly from the Damask. Into the Rose perfume went: Ginger Grass, *Aspalathos,* and Sweet Flag (or Iris). The plants were first steeped in wine, then mixed with the oil of Roses and a quantity of salt (twenty-three grams to eight-and-a-half gallons of perfume). The sesame oil was considered best for the base. Perfume was also obtained from the Rose from Phaselis (in Asia Minor) where it reputedly flowered all the year round.

Rose perfume was considered 'light', as was the Lily and the 'Kypros', as opposed to 'Khalbane' which was 'oppressive'. Although 'light', the Rose perfume was the most penetrating and destroying the scent of others. The attar of Roses was rubbed on statues made of wood to protect them from rotting.[48]

Rose petals were made into pomanders to mask the odour of perspiration.

Lily

Second only to the Rose in popularity, the Lily, royal emblem of the kings of Knossos (Crete), is much in evidence on Minoan frescos and vases. It had been cultivated from time immemorial, admired for its sweet, delicate scent and the pure whiteness of its petals. The Greeks traced the origin of this exquisite flower to the time of the birth of their greatest hero Heracles. Alcmene, his mother by Zeus, was so terrified by Hera's proverbial jealousy that she abandoned the infant in a field. Seeing his son exposed upset Zeus who turned to the goddess Athena for help. Athena invited Hera out for a casual stroll. It just so happened they came to the place where the infant Heracles was lying. Pretending surprise, she picked up the crying baby, and persuaded Hera to give him her breast to suckle, fully aware the milk of a goddess ensures immortality. Not paying much attention, Hera obliged. Heracles drew milk with such force that Hera cried out in pain and pulled the breast from his mouth. The milk spurted across the sky, forming the Milky Way. Where the drops fell on the ground, up sprang the Lilies.

The Lily became one of the flowers of Hera, wife of the supreme god Zeus, and through association with her the symbol of royalty and purity. The latter in no way contradicted the marital status of the goddess who annually renewed her virginity by bathing in a spring near Argos.

---

[48] Pausanias *Guide to Greece* vol. I p.401

The upright pistils of the Lily gave rise to phallic associations, making it an attribute of the goddess of love Aphrodite and of the permanently sexually aroused satyrs, hence symbolic of procreation.

In Chaironea (Boeotia), perfumes produced from the flowers of the Lily (in addition to the Rose, the Narcissus and the Iris) 'alleviated human distress'.[49]

Saffron Crocus

According to one story, the Saffron Crocus sprang from the blood of an infant called Crocus, accidentally struck by a disc while playing with the god Hermes. In another version the beautiful youth Crocus died of love for a nymph called Smilax and was changed into a flower bearing his name.

In yet another, it sprang from the warmth of the embraces of Zeus and Hera as they lay on their nuptial couch. Ever since it was used to decorate the nuptial beds of the newlyweds, additionally sprinkled with its scent, as the aroma reputedly made women more erotically inclined.

Saffron Crocus grew best when crushed well into the ground, writes Theophrastus. It also grew wild along roads and other well-trodden places. For perfume the best came from Cyrene, those from Aegina and Cilicia running a close second.

The Saffron Crocus was cultivated for a variety of uses in addition to perfumes. It was added to make up the incense, and also to flavour food. In cosmetics it stained nails and eyebrows and dyed linen fabrics orange. It had medicinal properties. Altogether it had been a much-valued plant from a very early history. Already the Minoans (c. 2,700 BC) used it and even had a Saffron gatherer featured on a fresco painted on one of their palaces. The Greeks continued to cultivate it throughout the following centuries.

---

[49] Pausanias *Guide to Greece* vol I, pub. Penguin Books 1978, tr. Peter Levi p.401

Spikenard

The Spikenard, known also as the 'Nard', came to the Mediterranean basin early in antiquity from the Himalayas, either via the Indian Ocean or the Silk Road.

Theophrastus was already familiar with it. The 'spike' or 'ear' which gave it its name 'Spikenard' grows from the rhizome. The oil used in perfumery for its musky scent was distilled from roots and leaves. It was one of the ingredients of the Royal Unguent (the others being Cinnamon, Cardamom, Myrrh, Cassia, and Ladanum). It anointed the brows of Parthian rulers and the brows of the very rich Greeks and Romans, particularly women.

This costly oil was also used to anoint the dead.

Violet

The Sweet Violet was probably the most popular flower in ancient Athens. Violet garlands and chaplets worn on festive occasions could be bought on Athenian markets even in the winter. On the first day of Spring, Violets were worn by children.

The most famous epithet for Athens was coined by the poet Pindar, who called the city 'Violet-Crowned'. He was referring to both the citizens and to the Muses companions of Apollo, who habitually wore Violet wreaths: 'O lyre of gold, Apollo's treasure shared with the violet-wreathed Muses'[50]. He then goes on to describe Athens of his day:

O glittering, violet-crowned, chanted in song
renowned Athens,
citadel of the Gods![51]

---

[50] Pindar, poet sixth to fifth century BC, *Pythian 1, The Odes,* tr. C. M. Bowra, Penguin, p.131
[51] Tr. C. M. Bowra *The Odes* Penguin XI

'Called you the town of the *Violet Crowned*', jeered the playwright Aristophanes, 'So grand and exalted ye grew/That at once on your tiptails erect ye would sit/those *crowns* were so pleasant to you'.[52].

The Violet (Greek *'ion'*) received its name when the nymphs of Ionia, who inhabited the banks of the river Cytherus, first presented it to Ion, son of Apollo and Creusa, the legendary ancestor of the Ionians. Its origin dates back to an incident involving a beautiful nymph who was transformed into a Violet to escape the amorous attentions of Apollo.

Another story tells of girls having an argument with Eros as to whether they surpassed Aphrodite in sweetness. Enraged by their impudence, the goddess first had them beaten black and blue, then changed them into Violets.

Violets were also believed to have sprung from the blood of Attis, lover of the Phrygian mother of all gods Cybele, who mutilated himself and died from his wounds.

The sweet- scented Violet perfume was considered very sensuous.

Galbanum

Galbanum grows in the Middle East and in Syria. The resin was used in incense and as an ingredient in perfumes. It was one of the ingredients of the Royal Unguent of the Parthian rulers.[53]

Ladanum

This shrub, native to Arabia, is the source of the dark-brown, bitter, fragrant Ladanum gum exuded during the summer months. It was collected by dragging a rake through the shrubs in the heat of the day when the exudations were at their peak, or by shepherds from the coats

---

[52] Aristophanes c. fifth to fourth century BC, *The Acharnians*, tr. Benjamin Bickley Rogers, OUP 1955; p.170

[53] *Dangerous Tastes* – Andrew Dalby, pub. The British Museum Press, p. 108-109

of animals and beards of he-goats. The gum had medicinal applications as a tonic and stomachic but was mostly valued for perfumes and burned as incense.

Storax

A small tree-yielding gum used for incense was obtained by making cuts in the branches. The gum is used in incense to this day.

Dioscorides noted that the gum had also a 'warming, mollifying, and concocting facultie'.

Terebinth

This tree yields the most fragrant resin of the native Greek trees. To this day it is the source of the so-called 'Chian turpentine', cultivated mostly on the island of Chios. The wood was used for dagger handles and for making cups which, according to Theophrastus, could hardly be distinguished from the pottery ones.

Aloe

It grows in India, writes Dioscorides, from where the extracted juices are brought. Perfumes were obtained from the resin.

Coco Grass or Nut Grass

Unguents based on oil kept better if thickened with powdered tubers of the Coco Grass. The Romans called it 'Radix Junci'. It is still used in India to perfume hair and clothes.

Cedar of Lebanon

Cedar wood was, and still is, used in perfumery. Logs were burned for their aroma. The aroma of the wood repelled pests and insects, hence it was used for lining coffers and chests for clothes.

The Cedar oil extracted from the wood 'has the power to corrupt living bodies and preserve dead ones, hence it is called life of him that is dead' wrote Dioscorides, because the smell of the wood drove away insects and worms. It was used to embalm the poorer dead, those who could not afford the Myrrh.

GILLIFLOWER OR STOCK – FLOWERS

Henna

The scent is obtained from the sweet-smelling flowers of this shrub native to N. Africa, Arabia, and India. The red pigment produced from the roots and leaves ground and dissolved in water was widely used in cosmetics, also to dye hair, nails, and fabrics. The Egyptian mummies were wrapped in Henna-dyed linen. The bark was used medicinally.

Jasmin

The sweet-scented fresh flowers were made into posies and necklaces, and as an ingredient in a popular perfume.

Quince

Theophrastus mentions the quince as the source of perfume – not expensive but popular. Unlike some perfumes to which a dye was added, the quince perfume retained its own colour.

Sweet Acacia

Flowers known as 'Cassie' are the source of a perfumed oil called 'cassie ancienne'.

INCENSE

It had been assumed since time immemorial that sweet fragrance and aromas were pleasing to the gods. Hence worship and prayers accompanied by suitable sacrifices were further supported by fragrant smoke from smouldering aromatic logs in order to gain greater favours. From the primitive resinous log fires of the dim prehistory, it was but a step for the subsequent generations to sprinkle onto glowing embers a mixture of aromatic herbs, gums, and resins for a richer result, leading to the makeup of incense. Very soon the temples and shrines of antiquity were filled with fragrant smoke from cakes of Myrrh and Frankincense carried on feast day processions and deposited on the altars of the gods.

The rising aromatic smoke derived from the resins, symbolically linking the earth with the heavens, the mortal with the immortal, explains its widespread and enduring use in places of worship. In funeral ceremonies it symbolised the ascent of a soul to heaven.

The ancient Greeks believed that incense and Frankincense burned constantly in the dwelling places of the gods. 'Perfumes always hover above the land [the Elysian Fields] from the frankincense strewn in deep-shining fire of the gods' altars,' wrote the poet Pindar, as did the lyric poetess from Lesbos, Sappho:

Come, goddess, to your holy shrine,
Where your delightful apple grove
Awaits, and altars smoke with frankincense ...[54]

It followed therefore that gods enveloped in those sweet scents would be recognised by a lingering aroma when they visited the earth. In the incident of the pirates intending to rob and kill the god Dionysus, whom they mistook for a rich traveller, they first became aware of an 'ambrosial' scent before the god revealed his divine powers and changed them into dolphins[55].

To obtain Frankincense and other fragrant resins, trading caravans went along the routes now known as the Silk Road. The Greek historian Herodotus noted: 'Towards the midday sun Arabia is the furthest inhabited land. This is the one country in the world where frankincense grows, and myrrh, and cassia, and cinnamon, and laudanum'. The caravans went even further, as far as the Indian Ocean. One source of precious gums known to the Greeks and Romans was in Sheba or Sabaea, a kingdom in Southern Arabia, another in the so-called Valley of Syria, but many remained shrouded in mystery and conjecture.

Of expeditions to discover the source of the resins two stand out. The Egyptian Queen Hatshepsut (the first woman to rule Egypt with the title of Pharaoh c.1,540 BC) planned a garden of incense trees for her mausoleum. With that in mind she ordered an expedition to the (then) mysterious land of Punt (present day Somaliland) from whence it returned with Myrrh and Frankincense trees. This achievement was commemorated on the reliefs in her temple. Centuries later Alexander the Great, perhaps prompted when still a boy by his tutor Aristotle, seized the opportunity once he became a ruler, to investigate their source by despatching a fleet to explore the coasts of Arabia.

---

[54] Sappho, poem 2, *Greek Lyric Poetry* tr. M. L. West, pub. The World's Classics, p. 36
[55] See "Wine"

Little wonder then that the aromatic resins and spices were a precious commodity in an ever-expanding market. Myrrh and Frankincense were valued on par with gold. The Assyrians took tribute of spices from the Arab kingdoms, as did the Persians – 'one thousand talents of frankincense per year', according to Herodotus.

Incense was used to induce prophetic trances through which gods spoke when consulted by mortals. The most famous example is Apollo's oracle at Delphi, where his priestess sitting in the inner shrine would fall into a trance and prophesy after chewing a bay (or laurel) leaf sacred to Apollo, and inhaling the smoke given off when sprinkled on the fire burning in the sacred tripod. Her more or less coherent words were taken down by priests surrounding her. Once composed by them, often in the form of hexameters, the god's response was delivered to the petitioners.

The Story of the Frankincense

Frankincense, one of the most important incense plants, grew in Arabia, 'the last inhabited land towards the South' as wrote Herodotus. It was the only country where it grew together with Myrrh, Cassia, Cinnamon, and Ladanum (derived from the leaves)[56]. On the Frankincense trees hung vast numbers of small, winged, multi-coloured serpents, guarding them. Nothing except the smoke of the Storax resin would drive them away. Those winged serpents were seen nowhere else except in Arabia, he was told.

The fragrant gum resin used to make the proverbially expensive incense was collected at the rising of the Dog Star[57] from incisions in the bark, wrote Theophrastus a hundred years later. Unlike Herodotus, who related hearsay, he had the advantage of the first-hand information from the reports of the Greek sailors returning from the exploratory expedition to the source of Frankincense and Myrrh ordered by Alexander the Great.

---

[56] Andrew Dalby – *Dangerous Tastes*, pub. The Br. Museum Press, p.113
[57] Sirius – marked the beginning of the summer

The Frankincense trees belonged to the natives, the Sabaeans. The gum was collected from the incisions in the bark, deposited on mats woven from palm leaves spread on the ground, scraped off, and brought to the Temple of the Sun guarded by armed men. The men who brought their gum crops to the temple placed them on the floor in a pile together with a tablet showing the price for which they were to be sold. The sales transactions were carried out by the priests of the temple, who kept one third 'for the god'. The rest was kept for the owner who came in his own time to collect what was owing to him. It should be noted the Sabaeans were honest and left the trees unattended. The Greek sailors who related the story to Theophrastus, however, were not. Seeing there were no guards about, they helped themselves to as much precious gum as they could carry and sailed away.

Frankincense, although very expensive, was nevertheless widely used, chiefly in worship, burned on the altars of the gods. The Elysian Fields were reputedly permeated by the scent emanating from the altars where they smouldered continuously. Offerings of Frankincense to the gods by the rulers of the day are frequently mentioned. The donation of Frankincense and other aromatic resins by Seleucus I, founder of the Seleucid dynasty to the Temple of Apollo in Didyma which he rebuilt at great expense, is but one example. The Egyptians proverbially used Frankincense and Myrrh in prodigious quantities. It was said one temple alone burned one kilo of incense in a day. 'In Babylon,' wrote Herodotus, 'on the altar the Chaldeans burn frankincense which is offered to the amount of a thousand talents' weight every year at the festival of the god'. Alexander the Great was reputed to lavishly heap incense on the gods' altars.

The origin of the Frankincense shrub is traced to a story of one Leucothea, daughter of a Persian king, who had fallen in love with the god Apollo and became his mistress. While Apollo was away their love affair was discovered, and Leucothea was walled up alive. Apollo returned too late to save her. As he sprinkled nectar and ambrosia on her grave, a Frankincense shrub sprung up.

The medicinal properties of the Frankincense were described by Theophrastus as 'heating' and as an antidote to poisoning by hemlock.

The story of Myrrh

Myrrh, one of the earliest recorded aromatic plants, grew in Arabia and East Africa, a habitat shared with Frankincense. Myrrh, noted Theophrastus, was the smaller of the two. The aromatic resin obtained from the bark was used in worship, in civic festivities and in perfumes since time immemorial. An Assyrian monarch had Myrrh shrubs planted in his garden, as did the Persian kings who inherited the Assyrian enthusiasm for gardening. In ancient Egypt Myrrh was also used in embalming. Herodotus provided the details: 'Brains were extracted through the nostrils ... the skull rinsed with drugs .... they take out the abdomen ... and fill the cavity with the purest bruised myrrh, with cassia, and every other sort of spicery except frankincense.' (This particular omission is not explained.) 'This treatment was for the rich dead. Poorer people were injected with oil of cedar.'[58]

Myrrh perfume was a luxury coveted by all. It anointed kings, it was worn as perfume (by women in particular), and it made precious gifts. It was one of the fabulous gifts brought by the Queen of Sheba on her visit to King Solomon. The Greek poet Theocritus added Myrrh to the list of the most exquisite items of luxury, of 'all that's best in life', that surrounded the handsome Adonis:

... at his side
fruit from the choicest trees, delicate plants
preserved in silver pots, rich golden phials

---

[58] Herodotus – *Histories,* Book II, 86, Wordsworth Classics, tr. George Rawlinson, p.150

of Syrian myrrh, fresh home-made honey cakes…
Theocritus: The Idylls; The Adonia - Singer[59]

The Myrrh tree features prominently in the story of an exceptionally pretty girl called Myrrha, daughter of a Syrian king Theias. Unwisely, her mother boasted loudly that her beauty surpassed even that of the goddess of love and beauty, Aphrodite herself. The goddess overheard it and was offended. In order to teach her a lesson, she inspired Myrrha with an incestuous love for her father Theias. Poor Myrrha! Burning with desire for her father who had not the slightest inkling of her feelings, she eventually tricked him by getting him blind drunk in order to make love to her. Once he discovered that Myrrha was pregnant with his child, Theias was seized with uncontrollable rage. He grabbed an axe and chased Myrrha, intending to kill her. She fled, weeping profusely, loudly imploring the gods for help. Aphrodite heard her, and repenting the mischief, just managed to transform Myrrha into a Myrrh tree before Theias caught up with her. In due course the tree split open to reveal a beautiful baby boy – Adonis. Aphrodite put him in a chest and took it to Persephone, asking her to look after the baby. But when she tried to claim him back, Persephone refused. The two goddesses quarrelled so bitterly that even Zeus himself was called in to intervene. In time Adonis grew into a beautiful young man and became Aphrodite's lover.

The Greeks always maintained the gum of the Myrrh tree was the tears of Myrrha, the unhappy mother of Adonis. Its tearful aspect was confirmed by Dioscorides: 'Myrrh is the Lachryma of a tree growing in Arabia wherein an incision is made, the teares distill downe upon the matts spread under.' He provides a long list of its medicinal properties – 'heating', sleep-inducing, astringent, good for sore eyes, falling hair, acne, to name but a few. Theophrastus noted that Myrrh scent kept well, ten years or more, the older the better.

Myrrh was also added to wine to give it a 'sting'. The Romans too

---

[59] Tr. Anthony Holden, *Greek Pastoral Poetry*, Penguin, p.104

spiced their wine with Myrrh, Cassia, and Saffron.

The Story of Balm

Balm or its resin, 'opobalsamum', is obtained from the tree of *Commiphora opobalsamum*. It was brought in antiquity to Palestine from S. Arabia, probably by the Queen of Sheba in the tenth century BC on her visit to King Solomon in Jerusalem. In the days of Theophrastus (fourth century BC) it was cultivated in Syria, in the valley of Jordan and in the Dead Sea region. Gum was collected from incisions made during hot summer days. Pure gum, noted for its exceptional fragrance, sold for twice its weight in silver, but if mixed, then according to its purity.

Pausanias had plenty to say about Balsam. He described it as a bush, the size of a Myrtle bush, with leaves similar to Marjoram. Vipers, whose favourite food was the Balsam sap, would hide there in search of shade. The Arabs who collected the sap were armed with sticks and rattles to scare them away, but did not kill them, considering them sacred and belonging to the Balsam trees. Also, they believed that feeding on this fragrant sap [60] reduced the strength of the venom, causing no harm.

Balsam sap was the source of valuable scent used in temples and in cosmetics. It was also valued for its medicinal properties, considered extremely 'hot', astringent, digestive, diuretic, and a poison antidote.

The Story of Cinnamon

Cinnamon bark was one of the most important ingredients in the composition of incense and scent. The perfume obtained from it was called 'Gizir' and smelled of roses. It was also valued as a spice and for its medicinal and preservative properties, as well as in cosmetics for skin

---

[60] Pausanias *Guide to Greece* vol. I, pub. Penguin Books 1978, p.367

discolorations.

The plant is one of the earliest ever recorded, mentioned in an herbal from Sumer dating from around 2,200 BC As 'Kasie' it was used in embalming in ancient Egypt. By the seventh century BC it was already popular in Greece as evidenced by an archaeological find in the sanctuary of Hera on the island of Samos.

Where it came from was not known in antiquity. Herodotus recounts a story he'd been told. 'Where the wood grows, they [the Arabians] cannot tell, they relate that [probably] it comes from the country in which Dionysus was brought up.'[61] (It might have been Ethiopia or, as Theophrastus later supposed, Arabia). In order to obtain a clean bark, the wood was chopped into small pieces and sewn up in raw hides where worms chewed up the wood, avoiding the pungent, bitter bark. He was also told how it was collected. Cinnamon grew in deep valleys and the people who went to collect it had to protect themselves against poisonous snakes. They did this by striking a bargain with the god of the sun, promising him part of the yield. The collected wood was divided into three parts. The portion that fell to the sun (presumably the one touched by a sunray) was left behind. On their departure they would see it go up in flames, as though consumed or accepted by the sun. 'Now this is sheer fable,' was Theophrastus' sceptical comment.

Herodotus quotes an even more fantastic story of large birds collecting the 'kinamomon' to build their nests on sheer rocks that were impossible to climb. The Arabians would leave pieces of meat near the nests for the birds to swoop down and gorge themselves on the meat until they were too heavy for the nests to support them, causing them to drop to the ground. The 'kinamomon' was then picked out of the nests by the men waiting below.

He mentions yet another way of collecting. It was supposedly located

---

[61] Herodotus – *Histories*, Book 3, 111, tr. George Rawlinson, Wordsworth Classics, 1996, p. 272-273

in a shallow lake, home to aggressive, winged animals prone to horrible screeching. Men had to cover themselves with hides of oxen and other skins to protect their bodies, particularly their eyes, before collecting it. These fanciful stories told to Herodotus were invented to protect the monopoly of a very lucrative trade.

Verbena – Verbena officinalis

The whole plant was burned in religious ceremonies for its aromatic smoke. The ancient Egyptians used it, hence its name 'the tears of Isis', an Egyptian goddess whose Greek counterpart was Demeter[62], wrote Herodotus.

---

[62] Her cult was brought to Greece in the third century BC

MUSIC

The Story of the Panpipes

Pan, the horned god of sheep and flocks, son of the god Hermes, passed most of his time frolicking with nymphs[63] on the Arcadian mountains. One nymph called Syrinx caught his fancy, but she rebuffed him and ran away. Undeterred, he chased her, while she kept calling out to her father, the river god Ladon, for help. Ladon managed in the nick of time to transform her into a reed. When Pan caught up with Syrinx, he found himself clutching a giant reed instead. He consoled himself by making a pipe from it.

Pan played it beautifully, and even challenged the god Apollo to a musical contest at which King Midas (of the 'golden touch' fame) was present. Although Apollo was judged the winner as always, Midas ventured the opinion that Pan's playing was better. His remark was overheard. As a reminder that gods do not suffer criticism lightly, Apollo changed Midas's ears to resemble those of an ass. Midas managed to hide them under a cap from everybody except his barber, who was sworn to secrecy. The barber, a simple fellow, could not hold out for long. He had to unburden himself somehow. Not daring to tell a living soul he

---

[63] Nymphs were not immortal but lived for several centuries. Some grew out of trees, the oak in particular, and died when the tree died.

went to a riverbank, dug a hole in the ground, whispered the secret into it, covered the hole, and went home relieved. But he failed to notice the reeds growing along the bank. Other reeds heard it and began to whisper: 'King Midas has ass's ears, King Midas has ass's ears'. The wind picked it up and Midas's disfigurement became known to all.

The pipes of Pan, or panpipes, became a popular musical instrument, indeed to this day. Theophrastus provided detailed instructions for making pipes from reeds. The most suitable time for picking them, he wrote, is June and July. The best mouthpieces came from the centre part of the reeds without plumes, which he called 'eunuch reeds'. A reed for the mouthpiece was ready for use three years after cutting. Reed tongues had ample vibration essential for those who play in elaborate style.

A boy called Calamus (whose name means 'reed'), son of the river god Meander, once challenged his companion, a boy called Carpus, to a swimming competition. Unfortunately, Carpus drowned, leaving Calamus inconsolable. In his grief the boy withered and became a reed growing by the riverbank.

Reeds had other uses as well. They were cut for stakes and arrows, and also used for weaving and plating.

SPINNING AND WEAVING

The Song of Linus

The pretty, blue flowered flax is the source of arguably the earliest fibre from which cloth was made. Its cultivation and harvesting are depicted in millennia-old Egyptian paintings. The wild variety was used since prehistoric times for its seeds and oil (linseed), but only later for its fibres to make the linen cloth. The oldest woven garment dates from around 8500 BC To obtain the fibres prior to weaving, the fruiting plants were cut, steeped in water to remove the soft tissue, then dried and bleached in the sun.

The plant was first imported to Greece from Asia Minor. Once acclimatised it was cultivated in mainland Greece, particularly in Elis where the soil was particularly good for flax and hemp. The best, according to Pliny, came from Cumae (Bay of Naples) where grew superb flax from which fine garments and hunting nets were made.[64] The Persians, wrote Herodotus, constructed ropes from flax fibres. When the Persian King, Xerxes (519-465 BC) invaded Greece, his huge army had to cross the Hellespont. He ordered a bridge to be built. It was done by lashing together ships with cables of papyrus and flax, weighing fifty

---

[64] *The Classical World* Robin Lane Fox quoting Pliny *Natural History* 19.10-11 p.35

pounds per foot.[65]

Weaving to make cloth was women's constant occupation. Servants, as well as high-born women, even the goddesses, were thus occupied, as mentioned time and again in literature and depicted on vase paintings. Penelope, the faithful wife of Odysseus, famously wove a shroud for her father-in-law, which she unravelled every night to put off her persistent suitors, declaring she had to finish it before making a choice.

The lovely goddess Calypso, who detained Odysseus on her enchanted island, spent time at her loom:

... singing high and low
in her sweet voice, before her loom a-weaving
she passed her golden shuttle to and fro ...

Homer – *The Odyssey*[66]

Linen cloth lent itself to a range of thicknesses. It was used for sails, shrouds, hunting nets, corselets. Men fighting in the Trojan war wore thick, protective linen corselets. Aias the Shorter, commander of the Locrians, Homer tells us, wore a corselet 'all of linen'.[67]

Linen breastplates were much appreciated by huntsmen as they broke the teeth of lions and leopards but were less protective in battle, being liable to give in under pressure from an iron weapon thrust into the wearer.[68] Dedicated linen breastplates were placed in sanctuaries. The Treasury at Olympia contained a number of them.

The versatility of the linen cloth is astonishing. At the other end of the scale, Homer mentions 'girls [who] wore robes of linen light and flowing,

---

[65] *The Ancient Mariners,* Colin Thubron, pub. Time-Life Books 1951, p.45
[66] Homer, *The Odyssey,* (OFTZ)Book V, 26-28, tr. R. Fitzgerald, Pub. Collins Harbill, p.95
[67] Homer *The Iliad,* Book II, tr. Robert Fitzgerald, Wordsworth Classics p.32
[68] Pausanias, *Guide to Greece* I, pub. Penguin 1979, p.60

the boys finespun tunics rubbed with a gloss of oil'.[69] The long Ionic tunics were made of fine linen (unlike the Dorian ones, which were woollen). Saffron-dyed linen garments were a luxury because enormous quantities of saffron were needed – around 50,000-75,000 flowers to produce one pound of saffron. Greatly coveted by Greek women, they were fit to be offered to the gods. 'This gift her gold-hemmed saffron gown Kleo gave Dionysus, dressing his statue ...' etc. runs one dedication.

Fine flax yarns were made into hairnets.

A popular myth, particularly in Argos, was attached to the flax plant. It was associated with the child Linus, a little boy exposed on a mountain by his mother, an Argive princess called Psamanthe, who bore him to Apollo but feared her father's wrath. While cared for by shepherds, he was killed by his grandfather's dogs. Betrayed by the grief she could not hide, the distressed mother was murdered by her father. Apollo stepped in and punished the city for the crime. The citizens were advised by the Delphic Oracle to propitiate the deaths of the mother and child by sacrifices and dirges to be chanted in their honour. Ever since it became an annual custom to choose a young boy to chant dirges at harvest time. The goldsmith god, Hephaestus, engraved a minstrel boy singing the story of Linus during grape-picking time on the famous Shield of Achilles. 'There was a boy singing the lovely song of Linus in a treble voice to the sweet music of his tuneful lyre.'[70]

In another version, Linus was the son of the Muse of Astronomy and Amphinares, son of Poseidon. He was a superbly gifted musician killed in a fit of jealousy by Apollo for rivalling his singing.[71] His death was mourned far and wide, even beyond Greece.

---

[69] *The Iliad, Shield of Achilles*, tr. Robert Fagles, Penguin 1991, p.487
[70] *Iliad* 18, 569/570, tr. E. V. Rieu, Penguin 1966, p.352
[71] PGG vol.I p.369

Basket making – Willow – Salix spp

Theophrastus listed several kinds of willow graded by the colour of the bark: black, white and red. For baskets the black willow was considered the best.

TREES

The soil of the hillsides of Attica was not suitable for trees to grow to a great height. New saplings had little chance against the ubiquitous goat, its appetite celebrated by a chorus of goats in a play by the Athenian poet Eupolis[72]:

On arbutus, oak, and fir we feed, all sorts of conditions of trees,
Nibbling off the soft young green of these, and of these, and of these;
Olives tame and olives wild are theirs and thine and mine
Cytisus, mastich, salvia sweet and many-leaved eglantine,
Ivy and holm-oak, poplar and ash, buckthorn, willow and heather,
Asphodel, mullein, cistus, thyme and savory all together.

This, coupled with the great and constant demand for timber, left Attica denuded of trees early on in history. Only a few forests were left by classical times, their loss already bemoaned by Plato (fifth century BC). 'There used to be abundance of wood in the mountains', he wrote in *Critias*, 'the mountains now afford sustenance for the bees, not so very long ago there were still to be seen roofs of timber cut from trees growing there, which were of a size sufficient to cover the largest of houses; and there were many high trees cultivated by man and bearing

---

[72] Eupolis, Athenian poet fifth c. BC, tr. Edmonds, *Garden Lore of Ancient Athens* pub. American School of Classical studies, Princeton, N.J. 1963 p.17

abundance of food for cattle'.[73]

Unlike the mortals, the gods had lush groves surrounding their temples and shrines where grew all kinds of trees. The goddess Artemis had a shrine in her sacred wood where grew the Cypress and the Pine. The sacred wood in Lakonia (S. Peloponnese) surrounded a temple to Ares, the god of war. On his feast day celebrated once a year, women were not allowed to enter the wood.

The gods guarded their woods jealously (with good reason) and punished severely any attempt at their destruction. Homer mentions an incident in connection with the famous Trojan horse instrumental in the fall of Troy. Having felled the trees from the grove of Apollo for its construction, the Greeks, mindful of the gods' wrath, established a festival called Carnea in expiation of the act.

Many statues of the gods were of wood with only the head and perhaps the hands of marble, stone, ivory, or gilded. A sanctuary in Kythera, for instance, housed an ancient wooden statue of an armed Aphrodite. Fig, Wild Pear, Olive roots, Cypress, Cedar (sometimes confused with Juniper) Oak, Yew, Boxwood – all lent themselves to be fashioned into the statues of the gods. Another popular one was the tropical Ebony, imported into Greece via Ethiopia. The statue of Apollo in Eleia was made of Boxwood with just the head gilded, Hermes had an eight foot one carved from Juniper, and the oldest statue of Hera was made from Pear wood. Asclepius, the god of medicine, had one reputedly made from the Chaste Tree (in spite of its name, more a shrub than a tree).

The trees themselves were also revered. Pausanias listed the most venerated ones in religious ceremonies. The first place he allotted to the Chaste Tree growing in the sanctuary of Hera in Samos, the second to the Oak in Dodona. The third place was shared by the Olive of Athena on the Acropolis and the Bay tree, the transformed nymph Daphne beloved of Apollo at Delphi.

---

[73] Plato *Critias* tr. Benjamin Jowell, from Wikipedia

Trees provided wood, an essential part of life, indeed to survival. Wood was used in a multitude of ways – house building, ship building, in military equipment, for chariot wheels, yokes, and in the home for cooking, heating, furniture, and tools.

TREES AND THEIR STORIES

Ash – Emblem of Strength

According to the Boeotian poet Hesiod, mankind inhabited the earth in stages. The initial Golden Age, when mortals lived like the gods, free from misery and toil, was succeeded by Age of Silver, followed by Bronze and Iron, each worse than the ones before. In the Bronze Age, people were formed from the Ash Tree. They were a brutish, nasty lot.

> *... All the Mortalls there,*
> *of wilde Ashe fashion'd; stubborne and austere;*
> *whose Mindes the harmfull facts of Mars[74] affected;*
> *And Petulant Injurie. All Meates rejected,*
> *Of Naturall fruits, and Herbes ...*
>
> *Hesiod: Works & Days[75]*

Apollo had a holy grove of this sylvan progenitor of mankind in Achaia[76].

The Ash wood was used to make spears. The spears were about six feet in length, the shaft bound with leather. References to Ash spears abound in the Iliad. It must have been superior to all other woods – an Ash-wood spear was Chiron's wedding gift to Peleus and Thetis, parents

---

[74] Greek Ares
[75] Hesiod Works & Days, *The Bronze Age*, tr. George Chapman 1618, *Oxford Book of Classical Verse* p.67
[76] PGG vol.I. p.243

of Achilles. Achilles put it to good use fighting the Trojans:

> *Now from a spear-case he [Achilles] withdrew a spear –*
> *His father's – weighty, long, and tough. No other*
> *Achaean had the strength to handle it,*
> *this great Pelian shaft*
> *of ashwood, given his father by the centaur*
> *Cheiron from the crest of Pelion*
> *to be the death of heroes.*[77]

Cedar of Lebanon

This is, without a doubt, the loveliest of trees, admired since ancient times. References to 'excellent cedars' abound in ancient literature. They could grow to an enormous size. A giant cedar growing in Arcadia even housed a wooden statue of the goddess Artemis inside it, worshipped as the Cedar Artemis.

Cedar wood was one of the chief exports of the Phoenicians, the denuded mountains of Lebanon a testimony to their indiscriminate felling.

The burning logs, and the oil extracted from the wood, were valued for their scent. The wood is also durable, resistant to pests and insect-proof, hence used in lining chambers and chests for clothes.

The Elm of Protesilaus

When the Greek expedition set sail for Troy at the start of that legendary war, it was prophesied that the first man to step ashore would be the first to die. Consequently, on reaching the Trojan shore everyone hesitated, apart from a Thessalian called Protesilaus, who leapt out killing many Trojans before, as foretold, being killed himself. He was buried with

---

[77] IFTZ, Bk XIX,386-392, p.348

honours at Troy where, according to legend, the nymphs planted Elm trees around his tomb. The trees reputedly grew only to a height enough for a man climbing on them to be able to see the walls of Troy, before they lost their leaves and withered. New saplings would then grow from their roots and the process would be repeated.

A grove of Elms was also planted by the nymphs around the barrow heaped by Achilles who killed Aetion and his seven sons in the Trojan War. A healing drug obtained from Elms growing near the graves of warriors who died of many wounds was supposed to be more potent.

The Hazel of Hermes

The Hazel belonged to a group of trees, Thorn and Rowan among them, believed to have sprung from lightning, hence containing fire, a quickening agent. All were regarded as trees of good omen, protective against witchcraft. When using the Hazel, a contact with the supernatural was sought through the god Hermes who, as the messenger of Zeus, was the mediator between the two worlds, moving freely among the mortals mostly on errands of Zeus, and conducting the souls of men to the underworld – women's souls were guided by the goddess Iris.

Hermes was a precocious god who lied, stole, and played tricks on the Olympian gods, which amused Zeus no end. Nevertheless, he felt Hermes had to be stopped from making mischief. After his solemn promise not to lie or steal again, he made him his personal herald and messenger. Hermes was given symbols of office with which he is usually represented – a broad hat, a pair of winged sandals, and a staff – the *caduceus,* made by the goldsmith god, Hephaestus. It was made up of an erect Hazel-wood rod symbolising the world axis and topped with two serpents wound in opposite directions forming a figure of '8', symbolising two opposing tendencies – beneficial and malevolent. Homer described the *caduceus* as a rod of prosperity and plenty. It had also the power to put humans to sleep and wake them up.

> *[Hermes] took the wand with which he charms asleep –*
> *Or, when he wills, awake – the eyes of men "[78]*

To be touched with the *caduceus* endowed a person with a range of powers, such as being able to express thoughts in words, to awake noble feelings of filial devotion, and to be inspired with reverence for the gods and love of mankind and country. Hermes gave a *caduceus* to the famous charioteer Pelops. It passed through several hands before coming into the possession of Agamemnon, leader of the Greek forces in the Trojan War.[79]

The *caduceus* was also an attribute of the god of medicine Asclepius, whose name means 'he who holds a magic wand'.

The Hazel was (and is) a great provider of nutritious nuts. Its rods were used (and are to this day) in divining for underground water.

Lime Tree

The Lime tree figures in the story of an old couple, Philemon and Baucis. Once, Zeus and Hermes decided to visit the earth in disguise. Everywhere they went they were refused hospitality except for this old couple who invited them to share their modest meal.[80] Before going back to his celestial abode, Zeus flooded the inhospitable village leaving only their cottage which he transformed into a temple where the old couple served as priests. He also granted them their dearest wish – to die at the same time. When it came, they were transformed into Lime trees. Ever since the Lime tree has been the symbol of true wedded love.

---

[78] IFTZ, Book 24, 315-89, p. 430
[79] IFTZ, Book II, p. 20
[80] See 11. 'Meals'

A Lime tree figures in the transformation of Philyra, mother of the wise centaur Chiron. She loathed the sight of her half-man, half-horse offspring and prayed to the gods to keep her away from him. They obliged by changing her into a Lime tree and, while they were at it, also named an island after her. The Argonauts sailed past it on the way to fetch the Golden Fleece.

Oak of Zeus

The Greeks believed the first tree to grow on earth was the Oak, and its fruit the acorn man's first nourishment. The Arcadians, described by both Homer and the poet Hesiod as the earliest inhabitants of the forests of Greece, were referred to as 'eaters of acorns'. To say a man had eaten of the acorns of Zeus implied respectable old age and experience. Acorns, however, were the food of necessity rather than of taste, quickly abandoned in favour of cereals and fruit. The poet Theocritus was to say this about it: '… acorn-husk falls short/of wild apple's taste; the one is sour, the other honey-sweet'[81].

The Oak forests were teaming with wildlife – boar, bear, wolves, and tortoises from which lyres were made. 'The Arcadians have different kinds of oaks in their forests – the broad leaf Oak, a "true" Oak, and one with spongy bark they call "Cork Oak" used for sea markers, for anchors and nets,' wrote Pausanias. The Kermes Oak which harbours an insect, was the source of a dye.

The Oak was Zeus's chosen tree for its commanding appearance which befitted 'the father of men and gods whose laws run both in the heavens and the underworld', to quote Homer. It is a tree that attracts lightning, interpreted as a sign of favour granted by the god of the sky, whose chief attribute was the thunderbolt. Zeus's other appellations were

---

[81] Theocritus: *The Idylls. V. The Goatherd vs. the Shepherd*, tr. Anthony Holden, *Greek Pastoral Poetry* p.68

'Cloud Gatherer', 'Rain-Giver' and 'Thunderer'.

An Oak tree believed to be frequently visited by Zeus grew in Dodona (Northern Greece) where thunderstorms were common. It became central to his cult there. Thunder was interpreted as the voice of Zeus, and the whole tree was credited with oracular powers. The rustling of leaves, cooing of doves nesting in the tree, the soughing of the wind in the branches, the sound of rippling water from a nearby brook – all were believed to be Zeus's utterances, made intelligible to his petitioners by a priestess who sat under it. When the wind rustled the leaves, people acknowledged the god's presence by exclaiming: 'Thus speaks Zeus!'

All kinds of questions were put to the god. Those preserved for us show concerns with common human affairs. 'Who had stolen my money?', 'Is the child my wife bore mine?' Others related to civic matters, such as a suitable location for a temple. Many prayers were for rain, this being under the control of Zeus, god of the sky. His priests dipped Oak branches in the brook while intoning prayers, giving rise to the belief among the Arcadians that rain could be brought down by dipping Oak branches in water.

An oracular beam from this tree was fitted into the *Argo*, the ship of the Argonauts, before they set out on their voyage to fetch the Golden Fleece. At its command, Jason and Medea had to be purified of the murder of her brother she had killed when pursued by her father's ship.

The ancient site of Dodona is set with the usual talent of the ancient Greeks, that is, in supreme harmony with the surrounding nature. Today only a few stones remain of one of the most ancient of Greek oracular cult centres. The stones are rough, the site austere, but then there was nothing gentle about Zeus. He wielded power regardless of human needs. The place where the oracular Oak grew is marked by a stone. Apart from the few young saplings here and there, those magnificent trees are now conspicuously absent. Yet something of the majesty of the supreme ruler of gods and men still lingers in Dodona, and the traveller leaves touched by its grandeur, particularly when the surrounding mountain peaks turn from violet-grey to indigo in the setting sun.

An Oak tree held sacred to Zeus figures in the 'Iliad' when Athena and Apollo transformed themselves into vultures and sat 'on a tall oak sacred to aegis[82]– bearing Zeus' to watch a battle. Homer mentions one Sarpedon who lay wounded 'in the royal shade of Zeus's oak'.[83]

Based on the association with Zeus, the Athenians presented crowns of golden Oak leaves to distinguished citizens. To be wreathed in Oak was synonymous with being awarded hero rites. The honour was so highly esteemed that replicas of the wreaths, made of thinner gold leaf, were placed on their tombs.

An Oak wreath was hung outside a house to proclaim the birth of a boy – there would be a woollen fillet for a girl.

At the festivals called Daedala, the people of Boeotia celebrated with great pomp the sacred marriage of Zeus and Hera in their aspects as the Oak god and goddess, represented by their images carved from Oak wood.

Apart from those belonging to Zeus, Oak woods were also held sacred to the corn goddess Demeter and the god of flocks and herds, Pan.[84]

Psychotherapy applied through memory regression has its origins in antiquity. Such was the case of a man called Iphiklos, renowned for his herds, who was impotent. He was cured by the seer Melampus, who managed to discover an incident in his childhood. When a small boy Iphiklos saw his father geld rams using a knife. Horrified, he ran away. The father, furious, drove the knife into an Oak tree. In time it was covered by the bark and it remained hidden until the seer found it, scraped off the rust and gave it (the rust) to Iphiklos as a potion. He recovered, even fathered several children.[85]

---

[82] Aegis – an emblem of Zeus, in a form of a thunder cloud, or a goat skin
[83] IFTZ, p. 91
[84] PGG vol.II, p.400
[85] C. Kerenyi *The Heroes of the Greeks* pub. Thames & Hudson, 1997, page 344

The Olive of Athena

The Olive tree came to Attica as the result of a contest between Poseidon, god of the sea, and Athena, goddess of war and wisdom, for its ownership. Poseidon made a salt spring gush out, while Athena caused an Olive tree to shoot up from the soil. The council of the gods judged the Olive tree to be a far more useful gift to the people of Attica and decided in Athena's favour. In sulky response, Poseidon flooded part of the land, but later relented and allowed the waters to recede. The grateful inhabitants named their city after her, dedicated a temple to her and stamped the coins of the city with her image.

The characteristic feature of this 'undaunted daughter of Zeus', goddess of wisdom and war, was the colour of her eyes, variously described as grey, blue-grey, grey-green and even sea-pale, obviously sufficiently unusual to merit particular attention. Her attributes were the owl, symbol of wisdom, and the Olive branch, symbol of peace, perhaps carrying a cautionary message that wars should be resolved peacefully. They were also stamped on the coins of Athens. Envoys suing for peace during military conflicts carried branches of the Olive.

An Olive tree sacred to Athena grew in the grounds of the temple on the Acropolis, dedicated to her. It was destroyed by fire by the Persians together with the temple, but immediately sprouted a four-foot green shoot. It brought hope to the citizens of Athens, who interpreted it as a sign of Athena's special protection of her city, particularly as at the same time another Olive shoot appeared by the altar of Athena and of Heracles in the Academy.

An Olive tree of proverbially long life continued to grow on the Acropolis. The place where it grew is marked to this day. The rebuilt temple, the Parthenon, a masterpiece of Doric architecture, was to become one of the wonders of the world and housed the famous gold and ivory statue of Athena by the celebrated sculptor Phidias.

Twelve Olive trees, reputedly from the cuttings of this acclaimed tree, grew in the grove of the Academy, where philosophers gathered and taught, famously Socrates and his disciple Plato. The playwright Aristophanes describes it in his play *The Clouds* where 'Right' says to 'Wrong': '... you'll run off to Academe's Park and relax under the sacred olive trees, a wreath of pure white flowers on your head, with a decent well-mannered companion or two; *[almost lyrical]* and you'll share the fragrance of a leafy poplar and carefree convolvulus, and the joys of spring, when the plane tree whispers love to the elm!'[86]

The oil from these trees, contained in special amphorae, were given as a prize to the winners of Panathenaic Games.

Cultivation of Olive trees goes back to the beginning of the Bronze Age and was well established by the end of it. The olive was (and is) the most important, indeed a vital commodity of Greece. The soil of Corinth was particularly good for the cultivation of crop-bearing Olives, their groves stretching right down to the sea.

Olive groves gave the Greek landscape its familiar appearance, lovingly described by the playwright Euripides contemplating the view of Attica:

> *... looking out on the hills olive-laden,*
> *enchanted, where first from the earth*
> *the grey-gleaming fruit of the Maiden*
> *Athena had birth...*
>
> *Island of Salamis*[87]

He was not to be outdone by the playwright Sophocles:

---

[86] Aristophanes *'The Clouds'* tr. by Alan H. Sommerstein, Penguin 1988, p. 153
[87] tr. Gilbert Murray, *Greek Literature in Translation*, Penguin, p.144

And there is a marvel here, I have not heard its equal
nothing famed in the vast expanse of Asia, nothing
like it in Pelops' broad Dorian island
ever sprang to light –
a creation self-creating, never conquered,
a terror to our enemies and their spears,
it flourishes to greatness in our soil,
the gray-leafed olive, mother, nurse of children,
perennial generations growing in her arms -
neither young nor old can tear her from her roots,
the eternal eyes of Guardian Zeus
look down upon her always,
great Athena too,
her eyes gray-green and gleaming as the sea.[88]

Instructions for planting and cultivating this invaluable crop, incorporated in the decrees of the lawgiver Solon (640-560 BC), specified that no tree could be planted less than five feet, (or an olive or fig tree nine feet) from that of the next proprietor. The trees come to full fruit bearing only fifteen to twenty years after planting. During the Peloponnesian war, the 'ravaging hand' of the Spartans razed the olive groves outside the city with a devastating effect on the economy and morale of the Athenians.

The fruit of the Olive formed part of the common diet. Oil was extracted from the fully ripened fruit harvested by shaking the branches with long, wooden sticks or long reeds. It was brought to the presses in baskets, then either crushed in a hand mortar or in a mill made of two stones or put into bags and pounded with a heavy wooden beam. The resulting oil was then poured into large earthenware jars sunk in the ground in front of the houses[89].

---

[88] Sophocles – *Oedipus at Colonus*, tr. Robert Fagles, Penguin Classics 1994, p.327
[89] Quoted from Richard Chandler, *Travels in Greece,* 1776

Oil was used for cooking, lubrication, lighting, medicine, and hygiene. Bodies were rubbed with oil, scraped off with strigils (many vase paintings show athletes doing this), rinsed off, and anointed with fresh oil, with or without fragrance. It was also used for preserving statues made of ivory, particularly that of the Olympian Zeus which cracked.

Barren olive trees were referred to as the scrub, whether wild olive, true olive, dog olive, and even a twisted olive. On the way to Epidauros, passing by a grove of wild olives, Pausanias came across a Twisted Olive growing by the roadside, believed to have been bent by Heracles himself into this odd shape. Perhaps it was the one that brought about the undoing of Hippolytus, the eponymous hero of the play by Euripedes, whose chariot reins became entangled in it, causing his fatal accident.

An Olive stake came to the rescue of Odysseus in one of his numerous adventures before reaching home, when he and his companions came to the land of huge, one-eyed cannibals – the Cyclops. The company made themselves at home in the cave of the Cyclops Polyphemus, the one-eyed son of Poseidon, while he was away tending to his flock of sheep. On his return he barricaded the cave, then, discovering the visitors, proceeded to consume a couple of Odysseus's companions, and more the following morning. Odysseus managed to save himself and the remaining men by blinding him with a huge Olive-wood stake lying in the cave, which he had toughened in fire. They escaped, undetected by the blinded Polyphemus, by lashing themselves under the rams as he let them out of the cave to their pastures.

An Olive tree played a crucial part in the reunion of Odysseus and his wife Penelope. After twenty years away, fighting in the Trojan War and subsequent wandering, Odysseus returned home to Ithaca disguised as a beggar. Penelope, not sure of his identity (and who can blame her, after all those years) put him to a test. Only she and her husband knew the secret of their marital bed, built by Odysseus on a trunk of a live Olive tree. As she said to her son:

If really he is Odysseus, truly home,
Beyond all doubt we two shall know each other
better than you or anyone. There are
secret signs we know, we two.

She suggested bringing the bed out for him. Odysseus replied angrily:

Woman, by heaven you've stung me now!
Who dared to move my bed?
No builder had the skill for that –unless
a god came down to turn the trick. No mortal
in his best days could budge it with a crowbar.
There is our pact and pledge, our secret sign,
built into that bed – my handiwork
and no one else's!

An old trunk of olive
grew like a pillar on the building plot,
and I laid out our bedroom round that tree... [90]

Thus convinced, Penelope fell into his arms, and a happy reunion followed.

The wood, very hard and durable, was used widely in carpentry, furniture, and domestic utensils.

The Wild Olive of Heracles

The greatest and the most famous of the Greek heroes Heracles, is best known for the Twelve Labours, though his exploits were many. His preferred weapon was a club he had cut for himself from a Wild Olive tree growing on the Helicon, a mount sacred to the Muses. Before he set

---

[90] Homer: *The Odyssey*, Book XXIII, tr. R. Fitzgerald, pub. Collins Harvill, p.p. 444 and 446

out to kill the Nemean lion, in one of the Twelve Labours, he described this club:

In my other hand a sturdy club of olive wood
its bark still fresh, its stem still moist, fashioned
from a spreading tree which I'd found by sacred Helicon
and wrenched from the ground, twisted roots and all.

> Theocritus: 'The Idylls'[91]

On a visit to Troezen, Heracles propped his club against an image of Hermes. It immediately struck root and grew into a tree. It was still there in the time of Pausanias who seemed somewhat doubtful of the story.

Heracles was in the habit of weaving for himself a wreath of Wild Olive. He was wearing one when he went to release Prometheus from the torture on the lonely mountain in the Caucasus.[92]

The Wild Olive wreath was the prize for which the contestants competed in the Olympic Games, established by him. Theophrastus reported a Wild Olive tree of remarkable old age in Olympia 'from which the wreaths for the games are made'. Centuries later, Pausanias also mentioned an Olive tree, called the Olive of the Beautiful Crown, from which crowns were made for the winners. Near it stood an altar to the nymphs (The Nymphs of the Beautiful Crown). The statue of Zeus wearing a Wild Olive wreath stood in the magnificent temple of Olympia dedicated to him.

The Palm of Apollo

The most famous Palm tree grew on the floating island of Delos. It happened like this. When the nymph Leto became pregnant by Zeus, his

---

[91] *Idylls* XXV, *Heracles and the Lion*, tr. Anthony Holden, *Greek Pastoral Poetry*, Penguin, p.140
[92] See Glossary

jealous wife Hera chased her all over the world and would not let her stay long enough in one place to give birth. Once Zeus became aware of what was happening, he anchored the island so that Leto could finally give birth to the divine twins – Artemis, the goddess of the chase and wild animals, and Apollo, god of light, reason, music, medicine, prophecy and archery, while supporting herself on a Palm tree. Ever since the Palm was held sacred to Apollo, and the island of Delos became the centre of his cult. Singled out by the god, Delos grew in importance both as a religious and as a political centre, housing the headquarters of the Delian League. In deference to Apollo, no birth or death was allowed to take place in Delos. Any pregnant or sick person was quickly transported to the neighbouring island of Rhenia.

A sacred Palm, reputedly an offshoot of the one that gave support to Leto, grew in Apollo's sanctuary by his altar. It was described by Odysseus when he met the princess Nausicaa in comparing her beauty to that of the Palm tree he saw there.

" ...So fair, one time, I thought a young palm tree
at Delos near the altar of Apollo –
I had troops under me when I was there
on the sea route that later brought me grief –
but that slim palm tree filled my heart with wonder:
never came shoot from earth so beautiful ...[93]

An annual festival was held in Delos in honour of Apollo, drawing delegations from various states. It was a great and solemn occasion celebrated with choral singing, sacrifices, and rich donations. During one of these, the Athenian statesman and general Nicias donated a Palm tree made of bronze. It was later overturned during a storm and fell on the statue of Apollo donated by the people of Naxos, knocking it to the ground. This incident was interpreted as a bad omen. Indeed, this turned

---

[93] Homer: *The Odyssey* Book VI, tr. R. Fitzgerald, pub. Collins Harvill, p.116

out to be the case. Nicias was one of the commanders of the failed expedition to Sicily. The defeated Athenians put him to death, blaming him for its failure.

Many Palm tree replicas were dedicated to Apollo in the course of time. One especially beautiful, donated by the people of Athens to the sanctuary at Delphi, his other cult centre, was recorded by Pausanias. The tree, surmounted by a golden statue of Athena, was made of bronze, the dates of gold. Unfortunately, it has not survived the passage of time.

Today a large Palm tree grows in Delos in the centre of what was once a lake and is now a reed-covered marsh. A row of the famous Naxian lions, in the so-called 'Terrace of Lions', line the way to the Palm tree. The rustle of its fronds in the sea breeze competes with the croaking of the frogs living in the marsh and in the cisterns scattered around the excavated area. Nevertheless, one can still recall the image that once inspired the poet Euripides:

The island hill of Delos
Shelter of Leto's travail
The cool grove of soft-tressed palms
Sweet-scented laurel and silver veil of the olive
That shades the curving waters of the lake.

From *'Iphigenia in Tauris'*[94]

In its heyday, Delos was a busy commercial port. These days, it is much frequented by tourists, arriving in boatloads for the day, from the neighbouring island of Mykonos. It remains uninhabited except for the keepers, perhaps in deference to Apollo's command that no one should die or be born on the island. With the departure of the last boat peace descends on the island as the setting sun pays tribute to Apollo, the embodiment of light.

---

[94] Euripides, *Iphigenia in Tauris, Chorus of Captive Greek Women*, tr. Ian Scott-Kilvert, *Greek Literature in Translation,* Penguin, p.153

Palms sacred to Apollo were also to be found on the island of Chios.

After having slain the monster Minotaur in Crete, the legendary hero Theseus sailed for Delos with his companions. On arrival, he broke off branches of the sacred Palm, distributed them among his men, and danced the Dance of Victory. Following Theseus' example, the Athenians presented Palm branches to victors of Panathenaic Games. Thus, the Palm became the symbol of victory, be it athletic, military, or spiritual, as well as the symbol of fame that comes in the wake of victory. As such, it became associated with the goddess of victory, the winged Nike.

The Palm was venerated by the Orphics[95] for its regenerative habit symbolising immortality, particularly the immortality of glory.

Palm trees were stamped on classical Greek coins.

The White Poplar of Heracles

In the famous Labour to capture the monster dog Cerberus, guardian of the entrance to the underworld, Hercules had to descend to the nether regions. Once there, he came across a Poplar tree growing by the Pool of Memory in the fields of asphodel. It was the unfortunate nymph Leuce, who once caught Hades' fancy, transformed into a tree by his jealous wife, Persephone. Heracles wove a wreath for himself from its branches before dragging the dog to the upper regions. In the course of the struggle the heat from his brows bleached the underside of the leaves which have remained white ever since.

White Poplars grew commonly by the rivers, streams, and ditches. Pausanias mentioned a resident 'woodman' at Olympia, whose job was to supply wood for sacrifices. Only the wood of the White Poplar, and no other, was used for the sacrifices to the Olympian Zeus because, as

---

[95] Orphism was a Greek mystical cult

Pausanias explained, Heracles brought the White Poplar to Greece which grew on the banks of the underworld river Acheron, and sacrificed to Zeus at Olympia, burning the thighs of the victims on the fire of White Poplar logs.

Based on the story of Heracles, who, having descended to the underworld and returned, had in effect conquered death, the White Poplar became a symbol of hope. It was held sacred to him and to heroes and athletes generally. The contestants in the Games on the island of Rhodos competed for a wreath of White Poplar.

The Plane Tree of Helen

The Plane tree reaches its natural Eastern limit in Greece. It grows by streams and rivers and was extensively planted for its dense foliage to provide a welcome shade, much appreciated in a hot climate.

> *I run from the sea and the earth more than ever*
> *is welcome to me, the wood's shade refreshing ...*
> *Give me sweet slumber beneath a leafy plane*
>
> *Moschus* [96]

Plane trees were planted wherever possible. In the Athenian agora (a place of public assembly and a marketplace) they were planted by the statesman Cimon. A Plane tree wood grew on the mountain in Pontius right down to the sea, sheltering the wooden statues of various deities. Many Plane trees grew in sacred groves. Pausanias visited one where he found huge, very old trees, hollow with age, big enough for guests to sleep inside after parties held there. The trunk of one such tree was preserved (or so it was believed) in a sanctuary in Aulis.[97] Plane trees can

---

[96] Moschus – *Lament for Bion*, IV, tr. Anthony Holden, *Greek Pastoral Poetry*, Penguin, p.191
[97] PGG vol.I p.285

indeed grow to great size. There is a record of one holding eighteen banqueters under its shade. Travelling in the S. Peloponnese, Pausanias came across a spring of pure water arising from a huge, hollow Plane tree the size of a small cave, providing the locals with good drinking water. It was called, appropriately enough, the Plane Spring. It was not unique. Huge Plane trees growing above water springs were common around Greece with sacrificial altars erected under their canopy. Odysseus refers to one in his speech to Agamemnon: 'We were sacrificing to the gods on their holy altar round a spring under a fine plane tree'[98].

Plane trees were admired for their beauty and often honoured. Jewels and fillets were tied round them, and wine poured on their roots which prompted some to comment: 'we have taught even our trees to be wine-bibbers'.

One splendid Plane tree was so admired by Xerxes, the King of Persia, on the march with his army through Lydia, that he covered it with jewels, stripping himself and his dignitaries of theirs, barely able to tear himself away. His love of Plane trees prompted gifts from his subjects. Herodotus recounts a story of a wealthy man called Pythius introduced to Xerxes as the man 'who gave thy father Darius the golden plane tree, and likewise the golden vine'[99].

The school of Plato was founded in a grove of Plane trees. It had belonged originally to the hero Academus, hence the name – the Academy. Plane trees were planted along the walks where teachers paced up and down with their disciples in deep discourse and where, as Aristophanes poetically put it: 'the plane tree whispers her love to the elm'.[100] The Lyceum had a tall Plane tree growing by a flowing stream.

The so-called 'School of Hippocrates' took place under a Plane tree on the island of Kos. The present tree growing in its place, replacing the

---

[98] Homer *The Iliad*, BookII, 358, tr. E. V. Rieu, Penguin 1966, p.48
[99] Herodotus *Histories* Book VII, tr. George Rawlinson, pub., Wordsworth Classics, p.526
[100] Aristophanes *The Clouds* tr. Alan H. Sommerstein, Penguin Classics p.153

one under which this Father of Medicine sat and taught, is estimated to be 500 years old.[101]

According to legend, Helen, the most beautiful woman of the age, was promised by the goddess of love, Aphrodite, to Paris in the famous Judgment. In order to claim his prize, Paris had to abduct her from her marital home, which precipitated the Trojan War. After the war Helen was reunited with her husband Menelaus and settled down to a quiet, domestic life in Sparta. She was subsequently worshipped as a tree goddess both there and in Rhodes. The Plane tree was sacred to her. Pausanias mentioned a Plane tree of extraordinary size and beauty reputedly planted by her husband, Menelaus.

Theocritus, the poet, confirmed the tradition of Helen's cult as a tree goddess in the poem 'Helen's Bridal Hymn':

But first we'll bind for you a clover crown
and set it on a plane-tree in the shade,
then we'll draw smooth oil from the silver urn
and pour our offerings beneath that tree.
And on its bark we'll write in Dorian,
For every passer-by to read: "Bow down,
For I am Helen's tree".[102]

In one version of the 'Rape of Europa' incident, it was not the Willow tree under which Zeus gratified his desire, but a Plane tree. Theophrastus reported a Plane tree in Gortyna reputed not to lose its leaves: 'and the story was that it was under that tree Zeus lay with Europa'.

The Plane tree was held sacred to the Earth Goddess on account of the shape of its leaf which resembles a hand stretched out to bless, a gesture with which she was associated. Its bark peels off every year and casts off

---

[101] See 16. Medicinal Plants

[102] Theocritus, tr. Anthony Holden, *Greek Pastoral Poetry*, pub. Penguin 1973, p.115

the dead tissue to reveal new growth, symbolising regeneration.

The many-headed monster Hydra, destroyed by Heracles in one of his Labours, was reared under a Plane tree.

Pine

The Phrygians worshipped the Pine tree, believing it was inhabited by the spirit of Attis, the deified Phrygian shepherd, lover of Cybele, the Great Mother of the Gods. She entrusted him with the care of her temple on the condition he would remain chaste. Attis broke the vow by making love to a nymph called Sangaris. Overcome with remorse, he castrated himself with a sharp stone while lying under a Pine tree and bled to death. The grief-stricken Cybele transformed him into a Pine tree and continued to sit under it in dejection and despair, until Zeus was moved to promise that it would remain green forever.

Attis, who died in midsummer, personified the passing of the Spring vegetation. The Pine tree, sacred to Cybele, played an important role in the rites performed in her honour. A Pine tree, representing the deified Attis, was cut down, bound with fillets, and decorated with violets believed to have sprung from his blood. It was then carried in procession by her castrated priests who slashed their bodies to the accompaniment of wild music. Intoxicated to the peak of frenzy by the music and the sight of blood pouring from their wounds, some participants likewise lacerated and even castrated themselves. Their blood and the severed genitals were then offered to the goddess and buried reverently in the earth. The festivities would end on a happy, even licentious note, celebrating the return to life.

A Pine tree figured in the tragic end of Marsyas, a Phrygian flute player, who challenged Apollo to a musical contest. Apollo consented on the condition the winner would impose any penalty he wished. He played the lute, Marsyas the flute. The contest was judged by his companions, the Muses. They were attributed with special functions of presiding over eloquence, epic poetry, history, pursuit of knowledge, dance, comedy, and tragedy, and took part in all great contests. Not surprisingly, they declared Apollo the winner. The god, whose patronage ranged from law and order to light and reason (his motto was 'nothing in excess'), momentarily forgot all he stood for, and had Marsyas tied to a Pine tree and flayed alive. Reputedly he hated the flute players thereafter.

A gruesome story relates to a robber called Sinis, allegedly a son of Poseidon, who lived in a region where Pines were sacred to his father. He earned his nickname the 'Bender of Pine trees' by catching unsuspecting travellers, tying them to the boughs of two Pine trees which he would bend down, only to let them spring up, thus tearing his victims apart. He was eventually killed in the same way by the hero Theseus (of the Minotaur fame).

During vintage feasts it was customary for girls to swing from Pine trees and hang masks on them in commemoration of the legend of Icarius taught by Dionysus the art of wine making, killed while introducing it to mankind, and buried under a Pine tree.

Pine wood had great many uses. It was used for timber, for fuel, to make tools such as mallets, in house, and shipbuilding. The 'Argo' of the 'Golden Fleece' fame was built from Pines reputedly felled on Mount Pelion, home of Chiron the Centaur. The triremes were generally made of Pine, the keel of Oak.

The wood yielded resin and pulp. The Pinecones, containing numerous edible seeds symbolic of fertility and fecundity, were thrown into sacred vaults during the annual festival in honour of the corn goddess, Demeter, together with cakes and pigs: 'to quicken the ground and the wombs of women'. The following year the remains were brought up, mixed with the corn seeds, and sown to ensure good harvest. Pinecones were also dedicated to the god Dionysus. They surmounted the god's *thyrsus* – the Ivy entwined wand, carried by him and his followers, the Maenads.

The Assyrians offered them to the gods who guarded life, a tradition carried on by the Greeks.

Medicinally, Dioscorides found the resin 'to help ye coughs and griefs about ye brest', and for boils and scabs in cattle. Asclepius, the god of medicine, was often portrayed with a Pinecone. Pausanias saw a statue of Asclepius in Corinth holding a sceptre in one hand and a Pinecone in the other.[103]

Willow

The Willow tree was the other tree to figure in the famous 'Rape of Europa' episode. Once Zeus, disguised as a docile bull, had carried the maiden Europa on his back and reached Crete, he shed his disguise and gratified his desire in a Willow thicket[104]. This incident, commemorated on coins from Gortyna in Crete, shows Europa sitting on a Willow tree.

A Willow grew by Hera's temple on Samos. It was believed to be the tree under which the goddess bore a child.

Persephone had a sacred wood in Phokis where grew Poplar and Willow.

In one version of the story about the Hesperides 'daughters of the evening', they were so devastated by the loss the golden apples Hercules took in order to carry out his eleventh Labour, they turned into Willow, Poplar, and Elm. This is probably unlikely, as the apples were eventually returned to their rightful owners.

---

[103] PGG vol.I, p.154
[104] See also 'Plane tree'

Ebony

The black wood of the Ebony was much prized for making statues of the gods. Its origin was unknown, only that it arrived via the Ethiopians. All kinds of stories were attached to it. A Cypriot proficient in medicinal herbs claimed the Ebony has no leaf or fruit, never sees the sun, and the wood is obtained from underground roots that are difficult to find. An Ebony substitute was the Rosewood.

ADDITIONAL NOTES

Cypress – The hard, durable wood of the Cypress was used in house and ship-building.

Fig Tree – The Fig wood which bends easily, was used in a variety of ways, mainly for chariot rails and wheels. Mention of its use is found in pre-Trojan tablets found at Knossos (Crete). The chariot of Lycaon, son of Priam, king of Troy, had a rail made of Fig wood, to quote one example.

Poplar (Black) – Populus nigra. Poplar timber, seasoned in water, was used for chariot wheels.[105]

---

[105] IRF Book 4,559-562, p.161

SHRUBS

The Laurel (or Bay) of Apollo

(Laurus nobilis. Its old name: *Daphne laureola)*

Not all of Apollo's numerous love affairs ended well, particularly that involving a lovely nymph called Daphne who caught his fancy. Daphne did not reciprocate his feelings, indeed she ran away from him, calling out to Mother Earth for help. Overcome with desire, Apollo gave chase, but the moment he caught her in his arms Mother Earth transformed her into a Laurel bush. All he could do was to break off a few branches to make a wreath and declare the Laurel sacred to him.

In Apollo's most famous oracle at Delphi, the Laurel was very much in evidence. The first temple dedicated to him was built from Laurel branches in the form of a hut perched over a cleft in the earth surrounded by Laurel bushes. The second was made by bees, from wax and feathers.[106] In the subsequent magnificent temple the priestess *Pythia* sat on a tripod above a cleft inhaling intoxicating vapours rising from it, chewing Laurel leaves, until she fell into a trance and prophesied. Her utterances were interpreted by priests surrounding her, who converted them into hexametric verses before handing them to the petitioners. In time, *Pythia* prophesied from an inner secluded cell of the temple where

---

[106] PGG vol.I, p.416

the only accessible opening was covered with Laurel leaves. The petitioners approached the altar carrying branches of the Laurel.

Those dew-moist roses and that bushy thyme
are sacred to the Muse of Helicon[107]
but your Apollo is the dark-leaved bay
which sanctifies your shrine on Delphi's height.

Theocritus *The Epigrams*[108]

A festival in honour of Apollo called the Daphnephoria was celebrated every ninth year in Thebes, during which a youth called Daphnephoros (Laurel bearer) carried an Olive branch adorned with Laurel leaves, topped with a shiny globe representing the sun-god, Apollo. Its origin was traced to a dream of Polemates, a Boeotian general, at the time of hostilities between Aetolians and Boeotians. Fighting had been suspended to celebrate a festival in honour of Apollo. That night Polemates dreamed a youth had presented him with a suit of armour. Three days later, the Aetolians were defeated. Polemates commanded the Boeotians to offer prayers to Apollo and walk in procession carrying branches of Laurel every ninth year.

Pausanias too refers to the Bay (Laurel) boys', so called for wearing Laurel wreaths, who were elected to serve as priests to the Ismenian Apollo. They were required (at least the well-to-do) to dedicate a bronze tripod to the god. The most famous tripod was dedicated by Heracles when he was a 'Bay boy'.[109]

The Laurel was also associated with Apollo's companions, the Muses, whose home was in a Laurel grove on the Parnassus, who were able to bestow the gift of artistic inspiration on the mortals while holding laurel in their hands. Laurel was considered to give prophets the faculty of

---

[107] The mountains of Helicon, as well as Parnassus, were the home of the Muses
[108] Theocritus *The Epigrams* I. tr. Anthony Holden, *Greek Pastoral Poetry*, Penguin, p.157
[109] PGG vol. I, p.329

seeing what was hidden. The diviners and priests of Apollo wore Laurel woven into wreaths.

The association of the Laurel with the god Apollo may have had an amorous beginning, but it went on to crown many distinguished heads to honour heroes, athletes, poets, and scholars throughout the ages up to the present day. The word 'Baccalaureate' (English version 'bachelor') a degree in higher education, has its origins from the custom of presenting wreaths of Laurel leaves with berries [baccae] to poets and scholars of academic distinction, as well as athletes. A wreath of Laurel crowned the winner in the Pythian Games, which took place at Delphi every four years. As explained by Pausanias: 'The crown for a Pythian games victory is a bay wreath, so far as I can see, because of the legend that Apollo was in love with Ladon's daughter [Daphne]'[110].

The Laurel was also held sacred to the god of medicine, Asclepius, by association with his father, Apollo. It was widely used in his temples for 'incubation', that is the induction of dreams to indicate a cure, and for acts of symbolic purification.

And I ... will sanctify
with laurel branches and holy crowns
Apollo's doorway and cleanse the floor
With splash of water
                    Euripides *'Dawn' (Ion dedicates himself to Apollo)*[111]

With the rise of Christianity, the powers of Apollo's most influential of oracles at Delphi waned, until it finally closed down in AD 390, followed by the destruction of the temple. This was the last message delivered by Pythia to the ambassador sent by the Roman emperor Julian the Apostate:

---

[110] Pausanias, *Guide to Greece*, tr. Peter Levi, Penguin 1979, p.423
[111] Euripides, tr. C. M. Bowra, *Greek Literature in Translation*, Penguin, p.149

Tell the king the fair-wrought hall has fallen to the ground.
Phoebus[112] has no longer a dwelling, or prophetic laurel,
Neither has he a speaking fountain;
The water of speech even is quenched ...[113]

The whole plant was put to a number of practical uses. Dry leaves were used in cooking. A soothing remedy was obtained from the oil of Laurel. The durable wood, able to withstand considerable wear, was used for drills to make fire, and for walking sticks. Allegedly it was the only bush preserved from thunder and possessed magic properties able to protect from misfortune.

The Myrtle of Aphrodite

The aromatic thick Myrtle bush was sacred to Aphrodite, the goddess of love and beauty. Before she took it over the Myrtle belonged to the gods Hermes, Dionysus, and the Graces. Pausanias saw a wooden statue of Hermes, almost invisible for the Myrtle branches. Powerfully scented, even endowed with magic powers, the branches were used for ritual sprinkling and for wreaths carried in processions.[114]

Aphrodite arose from the foam surrounding the genitals of Uranus[115] castrated by his son Cronus, who threw them into the sea. First, she swam to the island of Cythera, but decided it was not grand enough for a goddess, so continued further to the island of Cyprus which was more to her liking. Once ashore, she was received by three Graces who crowned her with Myrtle and Roses. Both plants became sacred to her. Myrtle bushes were planted by her temples. Wreaths of Myrtle were worn by participants in festivals held in her honour and carried in ceremonial

---

[112] Greek Apollo
[113] Delphi Oracle – quoted by Leonard Cottrell *Wonders of Antiquity*, pub. Pan Books London, 1964, p.163
[114] PGG vol.I, p.76
[115] A pre-Zeus deity, husband of Ge (Earth) and father of the Titans

processions. Through association with the goddess of love, Myrtle branches woven with orange blossom made up bridal wreaths.

Aphrodite supposedly wore a Myrtle wreath to the famous beauty contest judged by Paris, which precipitated the Trojan War. Presenting herself to Paris, she put on her magic girdle which made the wearer irresistible, promised him the most beautiful woman in the world and, not surprisingly, won. The unsuccessful contestants to the title of the "Fairest", Hera and Athena, hated the Myrtle ever since.

The extent to which Aphrodite was fond of the Myrtle is illustrated by the story of a girl called Myrene. She sought shelter in Aphrodite's temple from assassins who had murdered her family, and became her priestess. A young man fell in love with her. To prove it, he vowed to avenge her parents' death, which he did, and returned triumphant to claim Myrene. Aphrodite, however, was not disposed to let her favourite priestess go. She caused the young man to die and, just to make sure Myrene would always remain close, changed her into a Myrtle bush growing by her temple.

Aphrodite had a varied reputation. Mainly, as was only proper for the goddess of love, she was referred to as the 'Turner of Hearts'. But then Pausanias came across a sanctuary in Arcadia dedicated to 'Aphrodite the Contriver'. 'An absolutely right title,' he wrote, 'Aphrodite and her activities are the source of many, many devices and every kind of fresh resource of human language.'[116] This sentiment was echoed by the playwright Euripides (5th century BC) in his play *Hippolytus* where Aphrodite feeling slighted by the eponymous hero who worshipped Artemis, goddess of chastity, took cruel revenge.

On the other hand, Aphrodite was always helpful in matters of the heart. With this in mind Pelops, ruler of the Lydians and the Phrygians, sought her help when he decided to sue for the hand of lovely Hippodamea, daughter of Oenomaus. It was Oenomaus's condition that

---

[116] PGG vol.II, p.451

any suitor for his daughter's hand must win a chariot race against him, the loser to pay with his life. The race was made even more difficult by the presence of Hippodamea who accompanied each suitor to distract his attention. Thanks to Aphrodite's intervention, he managed to bribe Oenomaus's charioteer Myrtillus to pull the lynch pins from his master's chariot, win the race, and gain a wife. In gratitude he dedicated a statue of Aphrodite carved from a living Myrtle.

The city of Boiai in Lakonia (S. Pelopennese) traces its origin to a Myrtle bush[117]. Its future inhabitants wandering about, not knowing where to live, prayed to the goddess Artemis to show them where to settle. They saw a hare and followed it to a place where it hid under a Myrtle bush. This, they decided, was the spot pointed to them by Artemis and they built their city there. They worshipped her as Artemis the Saviour, and also the very tree when Pausanias who recounted the story was there. In Troezen (Attica) he came across a Myrtle tree with perforated leaves. 'The leaves were pierced with a pin by Phaedra tormented by love for her stepson Hippolytus'.[118]

Myrtle boughs were mentioned by Herodotus in connection with the Persian conquest of Greece. Before the army of Xerxes crossed the Hellespont, spices of all kinds were burnt upon the bridges and the way was strewn with Myrtle boughs.[119]

Wreaths of Myrtle were very popular with people going to banquets, in the belief they counteracted the effects of wine.

Boy, I hate their empty shows,
Persian garlands I detest,
Bring not me the late-blown rose,
Lingering after all the rest.

---

[117] PGG vol.II p. 84
[118] PGG vol.1, p61, and play by Euripides *Hippolytus*
[119] Herodotus *Histories* Book, tr. George Rawlinson VII,54. Wordsworth Classics 1996, p.535

Plainer myrtle pleases me,
Thus outstretched beneath my vine,
Myrtle more becoming thee
Waiting with thy master's wine.[120]

Horace – *The Ode to the Boy*

At an Athenian banquet it was customary after a meal to sing a song, pass a harp, or improvise a verse for amusement and entertainment. The most popular song was called 'The Myrtle Bough'. It celebrated the downfall of tyranny through the deeds of two men, Harmodius and Aristogeiton, who killed the tyrant of Athens with swords hidden in Myrtle boughs. The song reflected the intensity of feelings against any form of tyranny by honouring those men in song, statues, and liberties for their descendants, perhaps even surpassing their actual achievement.

I will wear my sword in a myrtle bough
Like Harmodius and Aristogeiton
When they killed the tyrant
And made Athens free ...[121]

The Myrtle, dedicated to Aphrodite and identified with the downfall of tyranny, fulfilled yet another role. Being evergreen, hence associated with death and grief, it was commonly strewn on graves. Myrtle reputedly lined the shady paths of the underworld where the disconsolate walk. Dionysus was able to bribe Persephone, the Queen of the Dead, with a Myrtle bough, in order to release his mother, Semele, from the underworld.

The Thebans held annual festivals in commemoration of the victims of Heracles, who killed his own children in a fit of madness sent by Hera.

---

[120] Horace: *Ode XXXVIII*, tr. William Cowper, *The Oxford Book of Classical Verse,* pub. OUP 1995, p.337
[121] quoted from J. C. Stobart *The Glory that was Greece*, pub. Sidgewick & Jackson,1971, p.110

In the funeral games that formed part of the ceremonies, the victor was crowned with a wreath of Myrtle. Thus, the Myrtle symbolises contrasting ideas – love and peace, grief and death.

It was important economically – Myrtle berries were highly rated by the Athenians, on par with figs and honey.

The Mastic of Dictyma

The Mastic was the favourite shrub of a virgin nymph from Crete called Dictyma, one of the attendants of Artemis, the virgin goddess of the chase, whose attendants were sworn to chastity. The Greek virgins adorned themselves with sprays of the Mastic in her honour. Through its association with Dictyma, the Mastic became a symbol of virginity and chastity.

A Mastic tree was chosen by the god Dionysus to manifest his power to defeat Pentheus, the King of Thebes. Pentheus refused to acknowledge the god and forbade his subjects to do so. In response, Dionysus caused his frenzied companions, the Maenads, led by Pentheus' own mother, to tear him to pieces, believing him to be a wild beast hiding in a Mastic bush.

Mastic grew widely in Greece and the Mediterranean, but the best came from the island of Chios, bringing considerable wealth to the island. It was cultivated for its aromatic resin, used to deodorise breath, and strengthen the gums.

The Cornelian Cherry of Geryon

Capturing the oxen of Geryon was one of the Twelve Labours of Heracles. Geryon was a three-bodied, three-headed monster, living in a far-off island in the West. His cattle were guarded by a giant Eurytion, and a two-headed dog Orthus. Heracles managed to kill both, then, when challenged by the owner, shot him too with an arrow. From Geryon's blood sprang the Cornelian Cherry, tinting its fruit red, the colour of the food of the dead. For this reason, it was held sacred to the death divinities. The witch Circe reputedly fed her swine on them.

The wood of the Cornelian Cherry was put to good use by the Macedonians. They made lances from it for their cavalry, and pikes, or *sarissas,* for their foot soldiers. The *sarissa,* fourteen to twenty feet in length, was made up of several pieces of wood joined by a tube of bronze, tipped with a blade of iron and fixed with a counterweighted butt. Men armed with the *sarissas* fought in close formation, called a *phalanx,* moving behind the cavalry charge, swishing them as they marched in step. Those who faced them, and lived to tell the tale, never forgot the sight.

The god Apollo was also fond of the Cornelian Cherry. He had one growing in a grove on Mount Ida, sacred to him.

CEREALS

Wheat – *Triticum spp.* – symbol of basic nourishment of body and soul

Barley – *Hordeum vulgare* – symbol of renewal of life and fertility

Rye – *Secale cereale* – cultivated since Bronze Age (domesticated remains found even in Neolithic sites). Some was grown by the Greeks, not much liked, added to make raised bread.

Demeter of the Threshing Floor

Some time between nine and ten thousand years ago, the hunter of animals and gatherer of acorns and berries settled down to cultivate the plants he had selected to ensure a steady supply of food. Exactly when and how he acquired this knowledge belongs to prehistory. Archaeologists point to various carbonised remains of cereal grains found in the Neolithic strata which revealed an established agricultural civilisation around 7,000 BC flourishing on the plains of Thessaly (Greece). Generally speaking, the remains of cereal plants cultivated at that time were identical with those of Asia Minor and the Middle East from where, it is assumed, crop cultivation first came. They included Emmer Wheat, Barley, Einkorn wheat and Pulses, already corresponding more closely to the cereals cultivated in the present times than to the wild varieties.

The Greeks held them to be a gift of life from the gods. The goddess of grain and fruits of the earth that they worshipped was Demeter. She gave the first year of the grain (probably Barley) to her mortal protégé, a boy called Triptolemus, taught him how to cultivate the crops, and instructed him to pass this knowledge on to mankind. The plain in Eleusis called Rharium was believed to be the first ever to grow crops, before it spread to the rest of the world. The Wheat and the Barley harvested there were used for the sacrificial cakes in the celebrations in Demeter's honour.

Demeter's attributes are Wheat sheaves. She is represented either holding them or wearing them twisted into a garland round her head. She might also be holding a horn of plenty (the *cornucopia*) to show that, as well as being a Corn divinity, she was also the goddess of the fruits of the earth and of abundance.

'Work on', the poet Hesiod urges his brother,
'so that Famine
will avoid you, and august and garlanded Demeter
will be your friend, and fill your barn
with substance of living... [122]

Demeter was worshipped both as a Corn goddess and as the mother of Persephone, referred to as the 'Maiden' or 'Kore'. Persephone was abducted by the love-struck Hades, god of the underworld, who carried her to his underground kingdom. Her sudden disappearance from the face of the earth plunged Demeter into despair. She searched for Persephone high and low, but only by causing famine was she told of her whereabouts. Thanks to Demeter's efforts, Hades was compelled to give up Persephone. Too late. By that time, Persephone had tasted the food of the dead, in this case the seeds of a Pomegranate, which condemned her

---

[122] Hesiod – poet/farmer from Boeotia c.700 BC; quotation from *Hesiod Tells His Brother to Work Hard*, tr. Richmond Lattimore *Greek Literature in Translation*, Penguin, 1973, p.57

to remain in the underworld. She was seen eating those seeds by one of Hades' gardeners, who reported the incident. The incensed Demeter punished him by changing him into an owl. In the circumstances all she could do was arrange for Persephone to spend only part of the year with her in the upper regions. Hence, during the thanksgiving ceremonies all kinds of fruit were brought into her sanctuaries, with the exception of the Pomegranate.

Persephone's travels from the underground kingdom of Hades to the upper regions of Demeter reflect the process of the germination of seeds in the ever-recurring cycle of the seasons. Persephone herself is the seed personified.

The joint worship of mother and daughter, Demeter and Persephone, was celebrated in one of the most important of all religious festivals in the Greek world. The departure of the Maiden-Kore was celebrated every October, in the festival called Thesmophoria, by married women only, and lasted three days. The participants had to refrain from contact with men and be chaste in mind and body. They ate Pomegranate seeds, flagellated themselves, and slept on branches of the Chaste Tree which reputedly cooled sexual urges and prevented immodest thoughts and dreams.

A grain puppet representing Persephone was buried in the ground for the winter. In the following Spring, at the festival of the Lesser Eleusinia, the germinating puppet was ceremonially dug up, celebrating her return to earth and the sprout of new growth.

By 600 BC the Greater Eleusinia, generally referred to as the Eleusinian Mysteries, were celebrated under official Athenian supervision. After purifications and sacrifices, a solemn procession made its way along the 'Sacred Way' which linked Athens with Eleusis. On reaching the sanctuary at Eleusis, the 'Sacred Way' wound its course among numerous altars. The actual 'mysteries', that is the mystic rites, took place in the sanctuary, where only the initiated took part. All women, free and enslaved, were eligible for the initiation. They assembled in a large hall able to accommodate up to three thousand people. At its centre stood a stone, carved in the shape of an ear of Wheat, symbol of Demeter. A grain of Wheat was displayed, to be contemplated in silence during the re-enacting of the mystic drama of death and resurrection. The obligatory fast was broken by the consumption of a ritual beverage – a mixture of Pulses flavoured by Mint. 'Sacred objects', presumably representations of male and female sexual organs brought in a basket, were uncovered, followed by the chanting of sacred hymns. What happened next was a closely guarded secret, its revelation punishable by 'ignoble' death. It has never been fully revealed but is believed to have included a ritual re-enacting of the death and re-birth of Corn, and through it, the mystic re-birth of the participants. Pausanias, who visited Eleusis in the second century AD, and who could have shed some light on the proceedings, was obstinately exasperating: 'The dream forbids me to write what lies inside the sanctuary wall,' he wrote, 'and what the uninitiated are not allowed to see they obviously ought not to know about'.[123]

Today, one can still admire Persephone's cave and the carefully preserved maze of ruins. Eleusis, however, being situated near Athens, is now surrounded by urban expansion, so that it is difficult to recognise the essentially agricultural cult for which it was once renowned.

Apart from the solemn celebrations, the most common and widespread forms of worship were the simple harvest festivals which took place at the local shrines where Demeter received thanksgiving offerings of the first sheaves of Wheat or Barley and the first fruits. 'We are on the way to the harvest feast,' declare three shepherds in a poem written two-and-a-half thousand years ago, 'some friends of ours are holding a banquet for well-dressed Demeter, loading her with first fruits, for she has filled their threshing floor high, the goddess, with rich

---

[123] PGG Vol.I (7), p.108

abundance of barley grain'.[124]

The worship of Corn deities cuts across the barriers of race, culture, and time. Fecundity and fruitfulness of the earth, being essential to survival, created the need to worship those gods whose concern they were. The framework of this worship has remained remarkably unchanged, pointing to the underlying unity of the human race in the search for religious expression. 'The modern student,' wrote J. G. Frazer[125], 'traces such resemblances to the similar and independent working of the mind of man in his sincere if crude attempts to fathom the secret of the universe and to adjust his little life to its awful mysteries.'

One of the basic elements of worship entailed the idea of sacrifice for the benefit and maintenance of life. In early, primitive societies, it often took the form of human victims whose blood, flesh, and semen were used to 'quicken' the earth in order to make it more fruitful. For the Greeks, the seed which needs to hibernate (in other words die) in order to bear fruit, was personified by the maiden Persephone descending to the underworld. Her worship was harnessed to her mother's, who embodied the concept of the subsequent harvest of grain and fruit.

Demeter's representations are many. The one in the British Museum is a statue of a seated matron, her face younger than the ample proportions of the rest of the body might suggest. There is only a slight aura about her hinting at the richness of autumn days as in that place she is of necessity one among a collection of distinguished works of art. To 'sense' her presence one should go, not unfortunately to Eleusis, or to a museum, but to a remote island, where the summer breeze strokes the ears of ripe Corn growing on terraced fields carved out from the stony hillsides. There, in the shade of a ripening fig tree, listening to the wind and the ubiquitous cicadas, one is reminded of the words of the poet Theocritus:

---

[124] Theocritus, poet fourth century BC *The Harvest Feast* tr. Anthony Holden
[125] J. G. Frazer – *The Golden Bough*

...I pray that I may one day plant again
the great winnowing fork in her heap of corn
as the goddess smiles her blessing on us,
with wheat sheaves and poppies in either hand.[126]

It would not do, however, even in such moments, to overlook Demeter's cult partner, her daughter Persephone. 'The cult of Demeter and Persephone was one of the few myths in which the sunshine and clarity of the Greek genius was crossed by the shadow and mystery of death'.[127]

Harvest festivals have not substantially changed in spirit, or indeed character, right up to modern times. A statue of Demeter was found in a Christian Greek village late in the nineteenth century presiding over a communal threshing floor. When it was carried away to a museum, the local folk were convinced they would never see another good harvest again.

OTHER DEITIES WORSHIPPED IN CONNECTION WITH HARVESTING OF CORN

In Argos (in the Peloponnese) the Corn deity was Hera, goddess of women and marriage. She was known there as the 'Goddess of the Yoke', and the ears of Corn were referred to as 'the flowers of Hera'.

Apollo, the god of light and sun, was offered the first crops of the season in his cult centres at Delphi and Delos, on the principle that the sun is necessary to ripen them. Among his many other aspects, he was also worshipped as the protector of crops from mice infestation and for driving away locusts at harvest time.

Athenian army recruits, obliged to swear the military oath, called

---

[126] Theocritus – *The Harvest Feast,* tr. Anthony Holden
[127] J. G. Frazer – *The Golden Bough*

upon a whole list of deities presiding over the staple crops of Attica[128] to bear witness – the spirits of Corn, Barley, Vine, Olives and Figs.

*

Only a small fraction of the Greek land was suitable for farming. The soil on the whole was poor and stony. The land, denuded of trees fairly early on in antiquity, did not retain moisture. What rains there were, mostly in the winter months, tended to wash away the remaining top soil, leaving the land even poorer. As if that were not enough, there was, and still is, the ubiquitous goat stripping off most of the vegetation within its reach. Hence, there was scarcely enough to sustain the population, necessitating reliance on import, mainly from Sicily, Thrace, and the Black Sea littoral.[129]

Most grain cultivation was confined to Barley, from which the staple food of the Greeks – the 'meal' or porridge was made. The districts where Wheat grew best were Boeotia, Thrace, and Pontus. Millet was cultivated widely, eaten in the form of porridge. Oat grew best in Mysia, but not considered for human consumption except in the times of famine. Some rye was grown in Thrace and Macedonia from which a rather nasty-smelling bread was made.

Farming in Greece was primitive and changed little with time. Crop rotation was unknown. Land was divided into furrows (about 130 feet long). The rough plough consisted of two pieces of wood, one end going into the ground, the other, pulled by a team of oxen or mules, made into a short handle to direct it. The ploughs were so unwieldy, and the ground so rough, that the fields had to be gone over several times and finished off manually. There were normally three ploughings a year.[130]

Homer provided us with a detailed description of ploughing: '... a large field of soft, rich fallow, which was being ploughed for the third

---

[128] Source: RFG, p250
[129] RFG p.126
[130] RFG, p 126

time. A number of ploughmen were driving their teams across it to and fro. When they reached the ridge at the end of the field and had to wheel, a man would come up and hand them a cup of mellow wine. Then they turned back down the furrows and toiled along the deep fallow soil to reach the other end'. The description of a king's estate follows: 'where hired reapers were at work with sharp sickles in their hands. Armfuls of corn fell down in rows along the furrow, while others were tied up with straw by the sheaf-binders. Three of these were standing by and the boys who were gleaning behind came running up to them with bundles in their arms and kept them constantly supplied'.[131]

The cereals were cut with sickles. Threshing was carried out with flails and sticks, sometimes chariots were run over it or trampled by mules or oxen. A splendid description is to be found in Homer:

> ...See in the mind's eye
> wind blowing chaff on ancient threshing floors
> when men with fans toss up the trodden sheaves,
> and yellow-haired Demeter, puff by puff,
> divides the chaff and grain ...[132]

The grain was collected in baskets and stored in large storage jars – amphorae. To make the flour, it was first crushed with rollers on stone slabs, then pounded in a mortar. A fairly coarse flour was obtained by grinding the resulting groats between two flat stones. The Greeks thanked Demeter for enabling them to dispense with the mortar by providing them with grinding stones to mill the flour. Pausanias in his travels came across a place called Alesiae (meaning 'a place of grinding') where a man called Myles was reputed to be the first man to use a mill and grind the Corn.

---

[131] Homer *The Iliad, XVIII, The Shield of Achilles*, tr. E. V. Rieu, Penguin 1972, p.351

[132] Homer, *The Iliad*, V, 490, tr. Robert Fitzgerald

In the days of Homer (around 800 BC) the mills housing the grinding stones were about five feet high. Odysseus reputedly had twelve such mills in Ithaca, his kingdom. Improvements to milling were made by cutting grooves into the rubbing surfaces of both stones, refined further by hollowing one of the stones so that the flour could fall out more easily. By the end of the sixth century, the upper stone was fitted with a wooden bar attached in such a way as to form a push-pull mechanism which made the operation easier. In Hellenistic times the water mill was invented.

When harvests failed, there was not enough food to sustain the population. Unable to live off the land, many people turned to trade and emigration. Not that the Greeks were keen, in spite of hunger and hardship, to leave their native land. In the case of an expedition forced by successive crop failures on the island of Thera, people were so reluctant to leave they had to be chosen by drawing lots, one per family. When they did go, it turned out to be a success story. On reaching the coast of N.Africa they founded the city of Cyrene in a land 'rich in corn, fruit and horses', which soon became renowned for its wealth.

MEALS

Food of early man came from the game he hunted and plants he picked. The first staple plants eaten by people living in the Mediterranean basin were asphodel roots, mallow leaves, and acorn mush. Regarded as the oldest settlers in Hellas were the Arcadians who reputedly lived even before the moon, eating acorns on the mountains at the advice of their king Pelasgos – not any acorns, only those from the oak trees growing in Dodona[133]. Acorns were put into woven baskets, crushed into a pulp using hot stones until a mush of acceptable consistency and temperature was obtained. Apparently eating acorns made people fat. In recognition, an acorn was stamped on the coins of Arcadia.

Acorns, however, were soon given up in favour of the more palatable barley from which a 'meal' or porridge was made. The grain was first roasted to remove the chaff, then ground and mixed with water and olive oil. It may not seem very appetizing but compared with the early diet of acorns it tasted well enough for the Greeks to be ever grateful to Demeter for providing them with grain. 'Blessed Queen of Heaven,' went a prayer, 'the original harvest mother who in joy at the finding of your lost daughter Proserpine[134] abolished the rude acorn diet of our forefathers

---

[133] PGG vol.II, p.370
[134] Greek: Persephone

and gave them bread raised from the fertile soil of Eleusis ... '[135]

Apart from the ubiquitous barley porridge, the Greeks ate bread as well. Bread was on the whole unleavened. A paste of flour and water was poured on a hot stone and covered with ashes. Sometimes it was left to get 'sour' to raise it. Varieties of bread were obtained by adding such ingredients as milk, honey, and wine. Often, wheat flour was mixed with barley but, for making bread of the raised kind, only wheat flour (and rye) could be used. In Athens there were bakers selling bread and cakes in the marketplace. Most of the baking, however, was done at home using the pestle and mortar to grind the grain to make the flour.

The art of baking bread probably originated in Egypt. The Egyptians discovered that when a mixture of flour and water fermented, it produced better, raised bread. According to Herodotus[136] they kneaded the bread dough with their feet. Whichever way it was produced, the Egyptians were able to boast of at least forty varieties of bread and cakes. They also improved the baking process by moving away from the basic flat stone heated from below to good working ovens.

Already in the Bronze Age, a variety of vegetables as well as corn were cultivated. Only in times of exceptional famine would people revert to 'the food of old time', doubtless a reflection on its taste. As Aristophanes mockingly wrote on 'The Gifts of Poverty': 'As to our Food, we shall exchange Bread for Mallow branches and Furmety[137] for the leaves of Radishes'.

The Greeks had one large meal a day, either before sunset or at midday. An everyday meal of an average Athenian would consist of barley porridge, olives, cheese, vegetables (most commonly beans, lentils, onions, garlic) and fruit in season. It might also include bulbs of gladiolus and asphodel pounded together and boiled. The sweetness

---

[135] Apuleius *The Golden Ass*, tr. Robert Graves, pub. The Penguin Classics, p.269
[136] Herodotus – Greek historian, c.484 – c.420 BC
[137] Hulled wheat boiled in milk with seasoning

came from honey and fruit.

Thanks to Homer, who paid a lot of attention to food, we know how people in his time banqueted. After a bath, dressed, perfumed and garlanded, the assembled company took their places on high chairs (the custom later changed to lying on couches). Then, to quote from *The Odyssey*:

> ... *a maid tipped out water for their hands*
> *from a golden pitcher into a silver bowl,*
> *and set a polished table near at hand;*
> *the larder mistress with her tray of loaves*
> *and savouries came, dispensing all her best,*
> *and then a carver heaped their platters high*
> *with various meats, and put down cups of gold.*[138]

Tables were changed twice, once for the meats, once for sweet cakes (usually barley cakes kneaded with honey) and fruit. This was the banquet of the rich, in this instance at the court of the king of Sparta – Menelaus. Another meal described by Homer was served at the court of Nestor, king of 'sandy' Pylos. Guests were first offered mulled wine accompanied by a side dish of onions. Honey and barley meal came next, followed by a drink of Pramian (i.e. the very best) wine, to which were added grated goat cheese and white barley meal[139].

At the other end of the social scale Homer described in detail a simple meal prepared by the swineherd Eumeus for Odysseus[140] whom he did not recognise and treated as a visiting stranger. He chose a hog from his herd, cut a tuft of its hair, which he sacrificed to the gods, then killed it and cut it up. He wrapped the pieces in fat, sprinkled barley meal, then skewered and roasted them. Once done, he offered one portion to the

---

[138] Homer- *The Odyssey. IV*,17-23, tr. Robert Fitzgerald, pub. W. Heineman 1961, p.67
[139] IRF Book II 742-758, p.317
[140] King of Ithaca, legendary hero of *The Odyssey*.

gods, one for the nymphs, one for the god Hermes, and the best piece, as a matter of courtesy, for the guest. Wine was mixed with water in a wooden bowl, libations were poured to the gods, and only then they began to eat, while a servant went round with the bread.

This was a special occasion to entertain a guest, besides, Eumeus had access to meat. On the whole, however, meat was eaten rarely. The urban inhabitants for whom it was expensive were on the whole limited to important religious feast days involving the sacrifice of animals.

In a ritual sacrifice to the gods, barley was scattered before the animals were put to the knife and a barley meal was distributed to the participants together with the meat.

The story of two old villagers, a shepherd Philemon and his wife Baucis, provides another detailed description of a meal offered to strangers. One day, Zeus and Hermes decided to visit the earth in disguise. Everywhere they went, they were refused hospitality except for this old couple who invited them to share their modest meal[141] where a special effort was made, dictated by the rules of hospitality.

First, they gave their guests warm water in a beech-wood bowl to wash, then spread a mattress stuffed with sedge grass on a willow-wood frame for them to rest. Baucis stirred up the fire with dry bark and leaves, followed by twigs hanging from the reed-thatched roof. The top of the table was wiped with stalks of fresh mint and set with beech-wood cups lined with wax for wine. Then followed clay dishes filled with olives, wild cherries preserved in wine, endives, radishes, cheese, eggs roasted in ashes, and slivers of smoked bacon sliced from a piece hanging from the rafters, boiled in water. All this was washed down with wine. For dessert there were dates, figs, and nuts arranged round a honeycomb. Still apologising for the poverty of the fare, they tried to catch their only goose, but it managed to escape.

---

[141] Ovid, *Metamorphoses,* tr. Mary M. Innes, pub. Penguin 1977, p.196-197

On the whole, the Greek cuisine lacked sophistication. The most delicious food they could think of – the *ambrosia,* food of the gods – reputedly consisted simply of barley porridge mixed with nuts and honey. Not that the Greeks despised indulgence. After all, the Sybarites, a by-word for luxurious lifestyle, came from a Greek colony in Italy.

At the other end of the scale were the communal meals of the Spartans, where the famous black soup consisting of pork and blood was served. 'No wonder they were so brave, if they can eat that they can do anything!' remarked their adversaries.

The present-day Mediterranean diet would not have been recognised by the ancient Greeks. Many of the popular vegetables, notably the ubiquitous tomato and the potato now taken for granted, were not introduced till hundreds of years later.

SPICES AND POT HERBS

There has always been the need to flavour food, even at the most primitive culinary level. The most basic and obvious was Salt. Other flavours to add interest to the taste and improve the aroma were obtained from seeds, roots, leaves, and bark of aromatic plants, generally referred to as 'spices'. Fortunately, the Mediterranean basin was well provided with aromatic plants, and many felt there was no need to look further. Leonidas of Tarentum, the Greek poet of the third century BC, praising the simple pleasures of home wrote:

Cling to thy home! If there the meanest shed
Yield thee a hearth and shelter for thine head,
And some poor plot, with vegetables stored,
Be all that Heaven allots thee for thy board,
Unsavoury bread, and herbs that scatter'd grow,
Wild on the river's brink or mountain's brow.

Yet, e'en this cheerless mansion shall provide
More heart's repose than all the world beside.[142]

---

[142] Leonidas of Tarentum, tr. R. Bland

With time, however, the Greeks (and the Romans) developed a taste for sharp, exotic spices which came from beyond the ends of the known world, brought by merchants along the shipping and caravan routes. It is doubtful if the consumers had even a remote idea of the source and origin of the spices they so coveted, such as Pepper, Ginger, and Cinnamon. The demand was huge and the trade too lucrative to reveal their places of origin. Indeed, they were kept deliberately secret, to the point of disseminating false information and spreading fantastic tales such as those told to the historian Herodotus and quoted by him in his *Histories*.

Among the exotic spices Pepper was king. Native of W. India where it grew wild, it was one of the chief imports from the East, brought in by Arab traders since at least fifth century BC The seeds, used for flavouring, were very popular and very expensive. Dioscorides recommended Pepper as a digestive stimulant. Theophrastus praised it for its 'heating properties' and also as a poison antidote.

A very expensive import to add zest to food was the Cinnamon, native of India and Ceylon, brought by Arab merchants. The Greeks flavoured wine with it as well as food. Fantastic stories were spun about its source to safeguard the monopoly and the revenue it generated.

Ginger, native to India, was one of chief imports of the Greeks. The aromatic rhizome of this luxury spice was used as a condiment, believed to stimulate digestion.

POT HERBS CULTIVATED FOR THEIR AROMATIC LEAVES AND SEEDS

Parsley

The funerary symbolism and decoration in garlands apart, Parsley was valued for its culinary qualities. It was eaten as salad or used for flavouring. Greek gardens were often bordered with Rue and Parsley, giving rise to the saying 'to be at the parsley and rue stage of the proceedings' implied their initial stage.

Wild Parsley gave its name to the city of Selinus in Magna Graecia (south coast of Sicily). Its leaf was struck on the coins of the city.

Celery

The seeds of the Celery, cultivated for its stalks, must be rolled and well-trodden in to give rise to a curly plant, advised Theophrastus. The whole plant was made into wreaths given to the winners of Nemean Games. It was stamped on the coins of Argos.

Marjoram

Fresh or dry leaves were widely used in flavouring. According to legend, Marjoram was created on Mount Ida by the goddess Aphrodite herself, hence the name given it – 'Joy of the Mountains'.

Once a youth called Amaracus, employed in the service of the king of Cyprus, tripped and dropped a vase full of precious ointments, spilling the contents. The terrified lad fainted. The gods saw the incident and were moved to pity. Before anybody could punish him, he was transformed into a sweet-smelling Marjoram.

Mint and Pennyroyal

Mint owed its existence to the transformation of a nymph who caught the fancy of Hades by his jealous consort, Persephone, who decided to transform her so that she could trample her underfoot. Mint appearing, as it did, in the underworld, is one of the plants of the afterlife.

In the upper regions, it added flavour to cooked dishes, particularly the ritual dish of Barley meal called *kykeon*[143] flavoured with

---

[143] RFG, p.171.

Pennyroyal, Mint or Thyme, consumed by the participants during the initiation ceremony of the Eleusinian Mysteries in honour of Demeter. The dish was also popular among the country folk, supposedly good for digestion.

Savoury

Considered one of the most fragrant culinary herbs, the flavour is obtained from the leaves and young shoots. The Savoury was planted near beehives to improve the flavour of honey. It was dedicated to the satyrs, who had a lascivious reputation. Married women, especially pregnant ones, were warned to leave Savoury well alone.

Southernwood or Lad's Love[144]

In connection with the sacrifices to Aphrodite, Pausanias mentions burning thighs of animals accompanied by a herb he called Lad's Love. He described it in detail – it grows nowhere but in Corinth, its leaves are shaped like an oak's, its colour is like that of a white poplar. Unfortunately, it is unlike the Lad's Love or Southernwood of the present-day Mediterranean flora, and so remains unidentified.

Thyme

Thyme was by far the most popular flavouring plant. Nothing was as tasty, no perfume as pleasant, as the Barley beverage, the *kykoon*, flavoured with Thyme, maintained a countryman going to the Athenian Assembly[145]. Thyme gives a particularly aromatic, sharp taste to honey for which Mount Hymettus was justly famous, from antiquity to the present day. In Thrace whole mountains were covered with the purple-flowered thyme.

Theophrastus noted that bees get their honey from the flowers and

---

[144] *Artemisia abrotanum?*
[145] RFG p.171, quoting Theophrastus *Characters* 4,2-3

that bee-keepers can predict the honey harvest from the amount of flower blossom. He also noted that Thyme cannot be grown where a sea breeze does not reach it, and for this reason it would not grow in Arcadia. This plant, he added, 'has been sought and obtained by those Athenians who wish to export such herbs'.

The purple blossom of the Thyme inspired many ancient poets. Theocritus wrote of 'those dew-moist roses and that bushy thyme sacred to the Muse of Helicon'. Thyme and the Mount Hymettus (Attica) were so closely associated in people's minds they became almost synonymous. The phrase 'to smell of thyme' denoted expertise in the Attic style of writing and praise for those who mastered its graceful elegance.

Balm

Cultivated for its lemon-scented leaves and lemon-like flavour, it was planted near beehives because 'bees delight in this herb', wrote Dioscorides. It was also a medicinal plant of high repute.

Basil

The aromatic leaves, fresh or dry, were widely used for flavouring dishes. Theophrastus wrote that cursing while sowing ensured germination. To make it grow quickly it should be watered with warm water in the morning and at noon. He noted it goes pale at the rising of the Dog Star, i.e., at the peak of summer

Coriander

The locally grown Coriander, a very ancient spice plant dating back to the Bronze Age, was widely used to flavour Barley porridge, and medicinally as a remedy for flatulence. Its name, 'Coriandrum' is derived from the Greek word for 'bug', suggested by the smell of the fresh plant when bruised. It was said the smell was so bad it made others smell better. The fruit used for flavouring lost this odour when dry.

Poppy

Dried poppy seeds were sprinkled on bread or mixed with honey as sweetmeats. The lyric poet Alcman mentions them in a poem: '... to each a table/bedecked with poppy-seed rolls, linseed and sesame, and bowls ... stuck with golden honey.'[146]

Oil was derived from the seeds. Pliny distinguished two kinds of poppy. He wrote: 'There are two kinds of poppy, white and black. The latter is cultivated for edible oil. The seed of the white poppy used to be served roasted with honey as dessert, and even nowadays peasants sprinkle it on loaves, using egg to bind it'.[147]

Poppies commonly found growing among the Wheat and Barley fields were believed to be mutually interdependent, the poppies providing them with a natural fertiliser.

Sesame

Sesame seeds mixed with honey were formed into small cakes or put into sweetmeats. They were also sprinkled on bread. Sesame cakes were traditionally served at wedding feasts.

Anise

The aromatic greyish-brown fruits with distinctive flavour were much valued by the Greeks, Egyptians, and Romans. Pliny recommended them to be taken in the morning with honey and myrrh in wine. Aniseed bread was considered a great delicacy.

Dill

One of the most ancient and a very popular culinary, medicinal, and decorative plant. Both the seeds and fresh leaves were used for

---

[146] Alcman – lyric poet seventh century BC, tr. M. L. West
[147] Pliny the Elder 'Natural History'

flavouring.

Cumin

Of all pot herbs this one, according to Theophrastus, had the most seeds. It was believed cursing and abusing it while sowing made the crop more abundant.

Mustard

The seeds were pounded with oil and vinegar to add zest to food. Its pungent taste sharpened the appetite and was considered good for digestion. Pythagoras thought highly of it for its effectiveness in clearing the brain.

Saffron Crocus

The orange three-branched style and stigma were used for flavouring cakes. Forty thousand blossoms yielded approximately a pound of dried stigmas.

Angelica

Preserved leaf stalks of Angelica were used to flavour 'sweetmeats'.

Bay (Laurel)

Dry leaves give a strong flavour.

Borage

Leaves were put in wine cups for flavour.

Sage

Leaves give a strong flavour to the meat. An important medicinal plant it was regarded as preserver of the human race, no less.

Rosemary

Fresh and dry leaves were widely used for cooking. It is also a source of oil and an important medicinal plant.

Fennel

The seeds have a pungent taste.

Juniper

The berries were used for flavouring meat.

Flavour obtained from the roots:

Elecampagne

The roots were used for flavouring sweetmeats and wine.

Liquorice

Dried roots were used for flavouring sweetmeats. An extract was obtained by grinding the roots into pulp, boiling in water, and concentrating by evaporation.

Horseradish

Cultivated for its pungent root.

VEGETABLES

The staple diet of the Greeks consisted of Beans, Lentils, Onions, Cabbage and Silphium, the last much valued but already extinct early on in history.

The Story of the Bean

This ancient, cultivated plant, considered to be one of the first fruits of the earth, wholesome and nutritious, formed an everyday staple diet for most people. Yet the superstitions surrounding it were many. The Greek philosopher Pythagoras,[148] who preached the doctrine of the transmigration of souls, emphatically forbade his followers to eat Beans. According to his tenet, Beans housed the souls of the dead who entered there waiting to be re-born once eaten by a woman. Bean seeds were thrown at ghosts to chase them away.

Pythagoras was not the only one. 'To eat beans was to eat one's parents' heads' is a statement attributed to Orpheus[149], who refused to

---

[148] Pythagoras,530-497 BC Greek philosopher, mathematician, strict vegetarian, associated with the doctrine of transmigration of souls
[149] Orpheus – legendary musician, founder of the mystical cult Orphism – its doctrines were contained in his poems

ever eat beans. Even to step on a Bean seed was regarded as trampling on a living being.

Prejudice against Beans had a long tradition, going back to the cult of Demeter who, while teaching mankind the cultivation of all kinds of grain, specifically excluded beans. The Pheneans in Arkadia who offered Demeter hospitality when she wandered looking for her daughter, were given lentils by her but no beans. Ever since, they believed Beans were impure.

Pausanias came across a small shrine on the road to Demeter's sanctuary in Eleusis. The shrine was called Cyamites, (i.e., of the Bean Man, derived from the word *cyamos* – Bean). 'I am not sure,' he wrote, 'whether he was the first to sow beans, or they simply named a hero like that because the discovery of beans cannot be traced to Demeter. Those that know the mystery of Eleusis and those who have read Orpheus will know what I am talking about. [150]

Even those who may not have shared Pythagoras's views or read the *Orphica* had an aversion to the Bean because it reminded them of a portion of a human body. Vegetarians rejected it on account of its red colour, which they thought was blood contained in the Bean, hence it was not a vegetable at all.

Some people went so far as to consider even touching a Bean as defiling. Certainly, the sacred king of Rome, surrounded as he was by many taboos, counted touching a Bean among them. Similar abstinence from the beans was reported by Herodotus in the *Histories*, on the customs of the Egyptian priests, who not only refrained from eating Beans but 'will not endure to look on, since they consider it an unclean kind of pulse.'[151]

Apart from those considerations, the Bean was also rejected on the grounds of health. Hippocrates considered it unwholesome and injurious

---

[150] PGG p.105
[151] Herodotus *Histories* tr. G. Rawlinson, Wordsworth 1996, p.132

to the sight, probably giving rise to the widespread belief, shared by the Greeks and the Romans, that eating Beans clouded vision. On the other hand, during the feast in honour of Apollo, the Pyanopsia (held during the month of October – *Pyanopsion*) a dish of Beans was offered to the god, mixed with flour and other vegetables.[152]

Yet for all that, Beans were eaten in considerable quantity, especially by the poor, a triumph of necessity over superstition.

The Story of the Cabbage

According to legend, the Cabbage sprang from the tears of Lycurgus, Prince of Thrace, who destroyed a vine plantation in defiance of the wine god, Dionysus. In punishment, the enraged god tied him to a vine stock. Lycurgus wept profusely. From his tears, as they hit the ground sprang Cabbages. This story may account for the belief that Cabbage was antagonistic to wine, hence good for a hangover.

Theophrastus distinguished three kinds of Cabbage: the curly leaved which had the best flavour, the smooth leaved, and the wild variety (probably a wild radish) which had a sharp taste and was taken for stomach upsets.

Garlic, Onion, and Leek

Garlic, Onion, and Leeks were part of the staple diet since the earliest times. The playwright Aristophanes mentions them in provisions for troops setting out to war. Each man was required to take with him enough provisions for three days which consisted of bread, Cheese, Onions, and Garlic, after which he was expected to live off the land.

'And the City would have been full of military preparations' with rations being doled out everywhere: people buying water bottle and jars and rowlock thongs at one stall, garlic, onions, and olives at another (*The*

---

[152] RFG, quoting Plutarch *Life of Theseus,* p.22

Acharians – Dikaiopolis).[153]

Both the Onion and the Garlic were supposed to promote courage in war. Garlic was given to cocks to make them fight better.

Various kinds of Onions and Garlic were named after the localities in which they were grown. According to Theophrastus, the best Garlic was Cyprian, used fresh in salads. Onions made a savoury snack to accompany wine.[154]

Onion and Garlic are mildly antiseptic, hence used medicinally. The Garlic may have been used in the 'Thesmophora', the annual feast in honour of Demeter celebrated by women only, who had to abstain from sex. It reputedly made their abstinence easier. In addition, the Garlic was endowed with magical properties, particularly as a charm against the evil eye.

The Leek was probably *the* favourite vegetable of the Greeks. It also had a number of medicinal uses – for warts, ring worm, as a purgative, as well as restoring one's appetite ever since it revived Leto, mother of Apollo and Artemis, when she was pregnant with the divine twins.

In addition, the Leek reputedly offered protection against lightning.

Lentil

One of the oldest leguminous plants native to the E. Mediterranean region is the Lentil. It grew fairly abundantly in Greece, providing a cheap, staple diet. Lentils were believed to be a gift from Demeter to the Pheneans (in Arcadia) in return for their hospitality when she wandered the earth in search of her daughter, Persephone.[155]

---

[153] Aristophanes, playwright, c. fifth to fourth century BC, tr. Alan H. Sommerstein, Penguin Classics 1988, p.73
[154] IFTZ II, *Meal at Nestor's*
[155] PGG, vol.II, p 409

The Story of the Silphium or Silphion

This famous plant, the *caserpitium* of the Romans, had already become extinct in antiquity. A wild vegetable, it flourished in Cyrenaica (N. Africa), most abundantly near Syrtis and in the Euspirides islands. It was mentioned by the historian Herodotus in *Histories*: 'The silphium begins to grow in this region (colonised by the Cyreneans) from the island of Platea on the one side to the mouth of the Syrtis on the other'[156].

Silphium resisted all attempts at cultivation or transplanting, and disappeared completely by the first century AD. While it flourished, it was of supreme economic importance. It made a sizeable contribution to the prosperity of Cyrene, based on grain, fruit, horses, but above all on the Silphium, which it acknowledged by stamping it on the city coins.

Theophrastus left a description of it. Its stalk was like a ferula in size and nearly as thick, the leaf like that of the celery, the fruit broad and leaf-like. It was eaten like Cabbage, and the roots were pickled. The stalk only lasted a year. In the Spring it sent up a leaf which purged sheep, fattened them, and made their meat delicious. The stalk, according to some, purged the body in forty days, others said it had a drying effect and aided digestion. Two types of juice were extracted – one from the stalk, the other from the root which had to be cut carefully, he warned, otherwise the unused juice would go bad. The sap was most precious, used in flavouring and medicine. Roots were covered with a barley meal to keep them from rotting in transport.

Dioscorides found many medicinal uses for it. It was excellent for digestion, effective for quickness of sight, thick throat, cough, dog bites, poisoned arrows, scorpion bites, and generally making people 'better coloured'.

It was also endowed with magic properties.

---

[156] Herodotus, *Histories 4*, Wordsworth Classics 1996, p.365

Mallow

The Mallow was an important food plant before the introduction of grain, or in times of famine. Leaves and stalks were eaten as vegetable or as salad.

The Mallow figures in the story of Oedipus, King of Thebes, the eponymous hero of the Theban plays by Sophocles. Having delivered the Thebans from a monster by solving the riddle of the Sphinx, he had unknowingly killed his father and married his mother, by whom he had four children. On learning the truth, he blinded himself and wandered out of Thebes, accompanied by his daughter Antigone. His tomb bore the following inscription:

Mallow above and asphodel I bear
My lap holds Oedipus, king Laios' heir[157]

Cucumber

The Cucumber was widely cultivated by the Greeks and the Romans. Praxilla, the Greek poetess of mid-fifth century BC writing on the pleasures of life, listed the ripening process of a Cucumber as one of them.

Loveliest of what I leave behind is the sunlight
and liveliest after that the shining stars, and
the moon's face.
But also cucumbers that are ripe, and pears, and
apples.

Praxilla[158]

---

[157] C. Kerenyi *The Heroes of the Greeks*, tr. L. H. Rose, pub. Thames & Hudson, 1997, p.104
[158] Praxilla, poetess, mid-fifth century BC, *Greek Literature in Translation*, tr. Richmond Lattimore Penguin, 1973, p.106

The best Cucumbers reputedly came from the district of Antioch. People of Megara covered their Cucumber and Gourd plants with dust during the Etesian winds (summer) to make them sweeter and more tender. The Cucumbers and Tomatoes that grow in the volcanic ash on the island of Yali have an unusual, sweet, and pleasant taste. Seeds first steeped in Cucumber juice before sowing apparently protected plants from insects.

Pea

Cultivated since Neolithic times.

VEGETABLES CULTIVATED FOR THEIR ROOTS

Asphodel

Cultivated mainly for the root rich in starch. Stalks and seed were also eaten.

Beet

Cultivated by the Greeks, it was eaten only as a vegetable, not utilised as a source of sugar which was then unknown. They distinguished between the black and the pale Beet, preferring the latter, particularly from Boeotia.

Corn Flag or Wild Gladiolus

If Theophrastus is to be believed, the root cooked, pounded, and mixed with flour, made the bread sweet and wholesome.

Tassel Hyacinth

The bulbs were cooked, 'though in some places they are so sweet they can be eaten raw', wrote Theophrastus.

Salsify

Also called Goat's Beard, alluding to its covering of fine hairs. It was cultivated for its roots.

Turnip

Known since pre-historic times for its edible root.

Globe Artichoke and Cardoon

The Globe Artichoke, well-liked by Greeks and Romans, originated in the Mediterranean basin. The edible part is the flower head and the fleshy receptacle at its base. The Cardoon was grown for its leafstalks, the roots were eaten, but less often.

Dodder

These so called 'vetch strangles' were eaten either raw or cooked.

Asparagus

Cultivated since ancient times for the young shoot arising from rootstock.

SALAD PLANTS

Chervil

A 'Herb of Joy'. In taste and appearance it is similar to Parsley, but daintier.

Radish

Theophrastus listed several kinds – the Corinthian was the strongest, the Boeotian the sweetest and round shaped, and the Thracian kept best in the winter.

Lettuce

Probably native to the Near East and cultivated for its leaves. Lettuce from Smyrna was considered the best.

Lovage

Cultivated for its leaves

Nettle

The young leaves were eaten

Chives

Foraged from the wild rather than cultivated

Samphire

Grows on sea cliffs on the Mediterranean coast. It was valued for its fleshy, aromatic leaves, and eaten as vegetable or salad

Rocket

Leaves were used for salad, and the seeds were the source of oil.

Hyssop

A culinary herb, also a tonic. Not much liked, it was considered bitter and difficult to digest, but nevertheless cultivated.

FRUIT

Fruit Trees of Dionysus

Fruit trees were placed under special care of Dionysus. Principally known as the god of wine and good life, one of his titles was 'Dendrites' (tree youth) and as such was worshipped as the 'Dionysus of the tree'. 'May the fields of the fruit trees receive an increase from gladsome Dionysus, the pure sunshine of fruit-time,' prayed the poet Pindar.

Presiding over the fruitfulness of the fields, flocks, bee keeping, and viniculture was his son by Aphrodite, Priapus, an ugly god with prominent genitals. He was worshipped as guardian of orchards and gardens. His image, or simply a phallus fashioned in clay, was hung on fruit trees to ensure divine protection and a plentiful crop.

Lamon, the gardener, to Priapos prays,
 Grant that his limbs keep strong and all his trees,
And this sweet gift of fruit before him lays:
The golden pomegranate, this apple, these
Elfin-faced figs, new grapes, a walnut green
Within its skin, cucumbers' leafy sheen,
And dusky olives, gold with gleaming oil –
To you, oh friend of travellers, this spoil.

Palatine Anthology[159]

The cultivation of fruit trees, estimated to date from around 4,000 BC, was well established by the time of Homer (seventh century BC), who provided a detailed description of Odysseus's Garden.

Having landed in Ithaca after years of wandering, Odysseus met his father who did not recognise him. And so, Odysseus described the garden given him to prove he was indeed his long-lost son:

I will tell thee also of the trees
through all this ordered garden, which of old
thou gavest me when I was but a child
begging for this and that, and following thee
all through the garden. 'Twas these very trees
that we were passing, and thou toldest me
the name and kind of each, and gavest me
thirteen pear trees, ten apple trees, and figs
two score; and fifty rows of vine as well
thou namedst as the ones which I should have,
where of each row ripened successively,
bearing all sorts of clusters, whensoe'er
Zeus' seasons from above weighed down on them.[160]

Fruit known to the ancient Greeks was much as we know it now. It was served as the last course, to finish off a meal, either raw, cooked, or preserved, that is dried (sugar was not known). Apart from Grapes and Olives, there were the ever-popular Apples, Quinces, Sorb, Pears, Medlars, Cherries praised for their flavour and stomachic properties, Blackberries, Raspberries, Black Mulberries (the white variety was unknown) and the fruit of the Strawberry Tree not in great demand (one

---

[159] Quoted from *Garden Lore of Ancient Athens*, pub. American School of Classical Studies at Athens, Princeton, NJ, 1963
[160] *The Odyssey*, 24, tr. William Morris, pp.304-312

was enough, according to the popular saying). Also the Plum, Damson, Pomegranate and the very popular Fig celebrated by poets. The Citron fruit was not eaten but used to preserve clothes from moths. Peaches were originally imported from Persia and rare, yet already by 400 BC they were being cultivated by the Eastern Greeks, evidenced by the find of a Peach stone in the shrine of Hera on the island of Samos.[161]

Among the most popular nuts were Chestnuts, Walnuts (sometimes referred to as the nuts of Zeus), Hazelnuts (or 'nuts of Heraclea' as, according to Theophrastus, the best came from there) and Almonds, for which in his time the island of Naxos was famous.

Although the overall patronage belonged to Dionysus, several fruits trees had individual associations with other deities.

Apple

Apples had been around since prehistoric times, testified by the carbonised Apple pips found in archaeological excavations in Anatolia dating from around 6,500 BC The Greeks had several varieties under cultivation, the Romans thirty-seven, listed by the Roman scholar Pliny (first century AD) in his *Historia Naturalis*.

The most famous Apple in the history of ancient Greece was the golden Apple that precipitated the Trojan war. It was triggered off by an incident at the wedding of Peleus and Thetis, attended by all the gods and goddesses except for one – Eris (Strife). Uninvited, she arrived all the same, and threw among the guests a golden Apple inscribed with the words 'To the Fairest'. Three goddesses – Hera, Athena, and Aphrodite – each felt the apple was meant for her. Unable to agree among themselves, they called on a shepherd, Paris, son of Priam King of Troy, who had a reputation for impartiality, to arbitrate. All three tried to bribe him – Hera with an empire, Athena with military glory, but when

---

[161] Robin Lane Fox *The Classical World* , Penguin, p.81

Aphrodite offered him the most beautiful woman in the world his integrity crumbled. Aphrodite, like a seasoned politician, gave away something that was not hers. The most beautiful woman in the world, Helen, was married. To claim her, Paris had to abduct her from her husband's home. His action sparked off the Trojan war, and the unremitting hate of the divine losers.

A tree bearing golden Apples, a wedding gift from Mother Earth to Hera, grew in the furthest Western corner of the world, in the Garden of Hesperides, 'Daughters of the Evening'. It was permanently guarded by a dragon, Ladon, who never slept. To bring back those Apples was one of the Twelve Labours of Heracles. He managed it by asking the Titan Atlas, who holds the celestial globe on his shoulders, to fetch them while he took over the burden. Atlas did bring them and was quite happy to leave Heracles to hold the earth for him. Heracles only managed to walk away with the Apples once he tricked Atlas to take the globe back, which he then dedicated to Athena. The goddess eventually restored them to the Garden.

Apple trees were believed to grow in the Elysian Fields where only the souls of the elect enjoyed a state of eternal happiness. A branch of an Apple tree symbolised the passport to paradise. It was carried by Nemesis, the goddess of retribution. While giving out to the mortals happiness and misery in equal measure, she also held out the promise of eternal reward. Pausanias mentions a statue of Nemesis carved by the celebrated sculptor Phidias holding an Apple branch in her hand.[162]

The fruit of the Apple tree was the symbol of love, probably on account of its shape suggestive of a female breast. It was sacred to the goddess of love Aphrodite. A gift of an Apple was no ordinary gift, it was a pledge of love.

---

[162] PGG.I, p.95

Girl: What are you up to little Satyr?
Your hand in my dress, fondling my breasts ...
Daphnis: Your little apples soft with down ...
I am giving them their first lesson in love."
Theocritus: The Idylls XXVII The Seduction[163]

A statue of Aphrodite in the sanctuary of Asklepios in Corinth was described by Pausanias. It was made of gold and ivory; the goddess held an Apple in one hand and a Poppy in the other.

Three golden Apples brought about the defeat of the heroine Atalanta. She challenged her suitors to compete in a foot race, the losers to be punished by death. A young man called Hippomanes fell in love with her and invoked the help of Aphrodite who was most obliging in matters of the heart. She gave him three golden Apples (not the ones from the Hesperides' Garden). Armed with them, Hippomanes accepted Atalanta's challenge. Every time she was about to gain on him, he dropped a golden Apple under her feet. Atalanta, intrigued, stopped to pick them up, which slowed her down enough for Hippomanes to win the race and gain a bride.

An Apple was also a symbol of renewal and eternal youth. During the search for the water of life in India, Alexander the Great came across priests who ate Apples to extend their lifespan.[164]

The Story of the Almond

According to Phrygian legend, as Zeus ejaculated while asleep on Mount Didymus in Asia Minor, from his semen sprang a monster with both male and female organs. The gods, alarmed at the sight, cut off its male organs and threw them away. On the spot where they fell, an Almond

---

[163] Tr. Anthony Holden
[164] Source: Mircea Eliade – *Patterns in Comparative Religion*, tr. Rosemary Sheed, London & N.York, 1958

tree shot up. In the Phrygian cosmogony the Almond, which flowers early in the spring before its leaves open, figures as the father of all things. The female of the castrated creature became the Phrygian Great Mother, the goddess Cybele.

The fruit of the Almond tree contained extraordinary powers. It was either eaten by Nana, daughter of the river god Sangarius, or she simply placed it on her bosom – and conceived! Her offspring was a boy – Attis who, on reaching manhood, became Cybele's young lover. On one occasion he was unfaithful to her. In remorse he castrated himself and bled to death. Through the intervention of the distraught Cybele he was transformed into a pine tree. From his blood violets sprang up.

The cult of Cybele and Attis involved ecstatic rites reaching heights of frenzy during which the priests (and some participants) mutilated themselves. It spread from Phrygia to Greece and Rome but was considered by many too extreme and distasteful. In Rome it was only officially allowed in the first century AD.

An Almond tree features in another, unhappy story. Acamas, son of Theseus, set out for Troy, leaving behind a girl he loved, a Thracian princess called Phyllis. When the war ended, Phyllis would come to the shore to wait for her beloved, watching out for the ships returning from Troy. As bad luck would have it, Acamas's ship sprang a leak and was delayed. After many futile visits, Phyllis became convinced he was no longer alive. Heart-broken, she took her own life. The gods were moved to pity and changed her into an Almond tree. When Acamas finally arrived, instead of flesh and blood he could only embrace the trunk of the tree. It responded by bursting into beautiful pink flowers.

The Sweet Almond is the source of nuts, while the Bitter Almond the source of oil.

The Story of the Date

The Date Palm is the source of the sweet, universally popular fruit, then as now. Dates came mainly from the hot arid regions stretching from Mesopotamia through to Egypt and Carthage. They were also grown in Greece but, as Pausanias pointed out, were not as tasty as those grown in Palestine. Dates formed part of the soldiers' diet, mentioned by Xenophon[165], leader of the 10,000 Greek mercenaries stranded in Persia, making their long trek home, He wrote: '… they arrived at the villages where the guides told them they could get supplies. There was plenty of corn there and date wine, and a sour drink made from boiled dates. As for the Dates themselves, the sort which one sees in Greece, were set aside for the servants, while the ones reserved for the masters were choice fruit, wonderfully big and good-looking. Their colour was just like amber, and they used to dry some of them and keep them as sweets. There was also available a drink which, though sweet, was apt to give one a headache'.

The top of the palm trunk – the 'cabbage' was also edible. Here, too, for the first time the soldiers ate the 'cabbage' and were impressed with its appearance and its peculiar, pleasant taste, though apt to cause headaches. Any palm tree from which the 'cabbage' had been cut off, not surprisingly, withered away entirely".[166]

The famous statue of Artemis in Ephesus represents the goddess with many breasts, identified as such only fairly recently. Previously, they were thought to be clusters of Dates hung on an apron, symbolising fertility and abundance.

---

[165] Author of *Anabasis or Persian Expedition*
[166] Xenophon (428-354 BC) *The Persian Expedition 3*, tr. Rex Warner,14-16, The Folio Society MMIX, p.52

The Story of the Fig

The Fig, one of the first cultivated fruits, was the most popular among the Greeks. They believed the Fig tree was given by the goddess Demeter to a man in Attica, Phytalus, in return for his hospitality during her stay on earth while searching for her daughter, Persephone. She also taught him how to cultivate it. Phytalus made good use of his gift. Not only was the Fig widely planted, but Attica became renowned for the quality of its Figs, considered superior to others. When Phytalus died, his grave bore the following inscription:

> *Hero and king, Phytalus here welcome gave to Demeter,*
> *August goddess, when first she created fruit of the harvest,*
> *Sacred fig is the name which mortal men have assigned it.*
> *Whence Phytalus and his race have gotten honours immortal.*[167]

The Fig came originally from Asia and was put under special protection of Dionysus. He was worshipped as the Fig Dionysus in Lacedaemon (Sparta) and on the island of Naxos, where he had an image made of Fig wood.

During the Athenian festivals, in his honour a procession of young girls of marriageable age carried Figs in baskets and a Fig wood chest containing a phallus, symbol of fruitfulness. They themselves wore strings of dried Figs round their necks.

In the early history of Athens, a number of people were kept at public expense to be used as sacrificial victims in case of calamity, such as an epidemic or famine. In the event two victims were chosen to be sacrificed, a man and a woman. The man wore a necklace of black Figs, the woman the pale variety. The fact that two persons were chosen indicates familiarity with the process of caprification, achieved by

---

[167] Quoted by Pausanias PGG (see Alternative translation by Peter Levy, Penguin Classics 1971, p.104

hanging branches of a Wild Fig carrier of gall insects, near the cultivated variety, to bring about pollination.

Scourging victims with branches of Wild Fig or Squill was also practised. In Asia Minor, an ugly or deformed man was chosen, given a meal of Wild Figs, Barley and Cheese, then beaten on the genitals. Beating human victims impersonating Fig trees on their genitals was believed to purge evil influences, release reproductive energies, and help the trees bear fruit.

By the time of Pericles (fifth century BC) the purification of Athens took place in the month of May (*Thargelion*) celebrating the *Thargelia* in honour of Apollo, during which two men carrying branches of Fig and bunches of Squill ran through the streets to drive out the grime pervading the city.

The goddess Athena received her due in the form of cakes of dried Figs after the ritual immersion of her wooden image in the sea.

Nuts and dried figs were showered on a bride during her wedding ceremony. A similar custom accompanied the acceptance of a new slave into a household.

A Fig tree became the centre of attention during a contest of the skill of divination between the soothsayer Calchas and the seer Mopsus at Colophon. Calchas challenged Mopsus by pointing to a Fig tree, asking him how many barrels of fruit it would yield. Mopsus gave an answer which was correct. He, in turn, pointed to a pregnant sow, and asked Calchas to predict how many piglets will be born. Calchas failed, and died soon afterwards of mortification.

Sweet, nutritious, and easily preserved (a great advantage in those days) Figs were very popular in Greece, growing easily in its poor soil. Entire armies fed on Figs. In the words of one poet, it was 'the god-given inheritance of our mother country, the darling of my heart, the dried fig'[168]. Leonidas of Tarentum, a third-century poet, was moved to write a poem in praise of a Fig tree:

A Fig Tree
Democritus fig-loving shouldst thou see,
Bear him this message, traveller from me:
The luscious fruit, maturely beautiful,
Weighs upon me, and waits for him to cull;
But fence is none; so, if he wish to taste,
tis fit that thou and he should both make haste.

(translated by Richard Garnett)

Dried Figs were supposed to bring about pleasant dreams, but green Figs, particularly if eaten at noon, could induce gripe and fever. Hippocrates was critical of the Fig. According to him it was indigestible, and he advised drinking a lot of water after eating it. Dioscorides, however, recommended it for dog and scorpion bites, toothache, and ear ailments.

The numerous seeds of the fig made it the symbol of fertility.

The Story of the Grape

The Grape is one of the oldest cultivated fruits. The vineyards had flourished in the Mediterranean region since antiquity. Grapes freshly picked were pressed to produce wine. Grapes dried in the sun, or buried in hot sand, were turned into currants. This is what Odysseus saw, when on his homeward journey, he was washed ashore on the land of the Phaeacians – an orchard planted with fruit trees and 'the vine fruit empurpled in the royal vineyard there. Currants were dried at one end, on a platform bare to the sun, beyond the vintage arbores and vats the

---

[168] Alexis – quoted in *Garden Lore of Ancient Athens* pub. American School of Classical Studies, Princeton, N J,1963

vintners trod; while near at hand were new grapes formed as the green bloom fell or half-ripe clusters, faintly colouring.'[169]

The Story of the Pomegranate

The origin of the Pomegranate can be traced to the story of Dionysus, who once fancied a nymph of whom it was prophesied will wear a crown. The foolish nymph thought this meant he intended to marry her and boasted about it. The wily god, however, changed her into a Pomegranate tree, twisting its branches into a crown, thus fulfilling the prophesy without getting entangled in matrimony.

The Pomegranate, with its numerous seeds, was a symbol of fertility, wealth, and abundance. It was sacred to Hera, patron deity of women and marriage. Pausanias recorded a huge statue of Hera he saw in the Heraeum near Mycenae, wearing a crown, with a sceptre in one hand, and a Pomegranate in the other. 'As the story of the pomegranate is rather secret,' he added enigmatically, 'I shall leave it out.'[170]

The Pomegranate with its red, fleshy pulp, the colour of the food of the dead, was also associated with Persephone in her aspect as a death deity. Carried off by Hades, once in his underworld kingdom she ate seven Pomegranate seeds. Having tasted the food of the dead she was condemned to remain there but released to the upper regions for part of the year thanks to her mother's intercession. Significantly, the Arcadians brought every kind of cultivated fruit to the sanctuary of Demeter except the Pomegranate, whose seeds had doomed her daughter to the underworld. Thus, the Pomegranate symbolises both death and plenty.

A story from the city of Side in Asia Minor tells of a widower who was about to seduce his own daughter Side. To escape his attentions, she killed herself. The gods transformed her into a Pomegranate tree and her

---

[169] OFTZVII, p.126
[170] PGG.I, p.170

father into a sparrow hawk which, it was believed, would never alight on it. Whether to commemorate this incident or simply as the symbol of fertility, the Pomegranate was stamped on the coins of the city.

The Greeks were very fond of Pomegranates. The best reputedly came from Attica and Boeotia. The rind was used in tanning and dyeing.

The Story of the Pear

The Pear was sacred to Hera, both wife and sister of Zeus, patron divinity of women and marriage, famed for jealousy and vindictiveness. The most ancient statues of her were made of Pear wood. Pausanias mentioned one such statue – a small, seated image dedicated in Tiryns, in her temple, the Heraeum.

A sacred Pear tree grew in the precincts of the Heraeum on the island of Samos, her birthplace. No Pear tree grows there now. All that remains of the once magnificent temple is a jumble of stones, the result not only of the passage of time, but also of rebuilding and alterations carried out in antiquity. It is nevertheless possible to make out the size and the former splendour of the temple, a testimony to the grand schemes of the famous tyrant (i.e., ruler) of Samos, Polycrates. It is situated between the mountains and the sea shore, in perfect harmony with its surroundings for which the Greeks were famous.

How did it come about for this vengeful goddess to inspire men to dedicate such grand monuments to her? There was nothing kind about Hera. When she did show concern, it was usually with an ulterior motive, or sheer spite. No slights were ever forgiven or forgotten. Yet mankind sought her gentler side by making her the patroness of women and invited her to walk among the shaded colonnades fingering Pear blossom shaken by the mountain breeze.

The distinctive shape of the Pear fruit made it also sacred to Aphrodite-Columella. It was called the *Pyrus venera* – the Pear of (erotic) love.

The Story of the Quince

The Quince, like the Apple, was sacred to Aphrodite. In the processions celebrated in her honour, chariots were filled with flowers and fruit sacred to her – Myrtle, Roses, Apples, and Quinces. Through association with the goddess of love, the Quince became the symbol of married love. During a marriage ceremony, a Greek bride was bound by the decree of Solon to eat a cake and a Quince before going to her newly wedded husband's hearth. The wedding cake of Sesame and Honey served during the ceremony contained the Quince, symbolic of fecundity.

The Quince was highly valued in its own right, as a fruit to be eaten. It can keep fresh for a long time, very important in those days. It even inspired poets. The Greek poet Antiphilus wrote a poem on a Quince preserved through the winter, given to a lady:

I am a quince, saved over from last year, still fresh
my skin young, not spotted or wrinkled, downy as the new-born,
as though I were still among my leaves. Seldom
does winter yield such gifts, but for you, my queen,
even the snows and frosts bear harvests like this.[171]

There is a story involving the Quince, its moral being that a trick played at the right moment can overcome the most formidable odds. Once a young man, called Acontius, fell in love with a beautiful girl Cydippe. He noticed her while she attended a religious ceremony in honour of the goddess Artemis. Having discovered she came from a family far above his own, he realised his offer of marriage was bound to be rejected. He thought of a trick that might improve his chances. While she performed devotions in the temple, he threw a Quince at her feet on which he wrote an inscription. The puzzled girl picked it up and read it aloud: 'I swear by the divinity of Artemis to become the wife of

---

[171] Tr. W. S. Mervin

Acontius'. Compelled by the oath taken in the divine presence, albeit inadvertently, she became his wife.

ADDITIONAL NOTES

Almond

Bitter Almond is the source of oil; Sweet Almond is grown for nuts

Cherry

To make the famous Trojan horse, which brought an end to the Trojan War, the Greeks chopped down a Wild Cherry tree growing in the sacred grove of Apollo, incurring his wrath. To placate him they erected an altar to the Apollo of the Cherry, where sacrifices were performed.

The fruit of the Cherry was very popular indeed.

Strawberry tree

Native to the Mediterranean region, the shrub has an attractive-looking fruit, unfortunately not very tasty. According to an old saying, 'one was enough'. The Strawberry Trees growing on the mountains of Helicon, home of the Muses, were reputedly the best – for goats.

Walnut

Artemis, the goddess chiefly of hunt and chastity, had many other aspects as well. As Artemis Caryatis she took the form of a Walnut tree rich in nuts and endowed it with second sight, linking the Walnut with the gift of prophesy.[172]

---

[172]Pierre Grimal: *Dictionnaire de la mythologie grecque et romaine*, 3rd corrected edition, Paris 1963, p.126

Ziziphus or Common Jujube

The fruit of this spiny shrub is sweeter if one pours wine over it – as advised by Theophrastus.

Citron

Nowadays it is hard to imagine the Mediterranean landscape without groves of Orange and Lemon trees, yet they were not cultivated in antiquity. One of the first fruits to come from the East to the Mediterranean, around 300 BC was the citron, an elongated fruit with a thick skin and a fleshy pulp. The fruit was not considered good to eat, but together with the leaf, was noted for the fragrance. It was placed in coffers among clothes to drive away moths.

WINE

The Story of Wine and the Cult of Dionysus

Known principally as the god of wine, Dionysus came from Thrace and had to conquer the Greek world before being reluctantly accepted into the clan of the Olympian gods.[173] His birth and adolescence were nothing short of dramatic. He was the offspring of the union of the supreme god Zeus and a mortal daughter of the king of Thebes, Semele. While pregnant, Semele was seized with the desire to see her lover Zeus without his habitual disguise of a mortal man. Much against his wish, Zeus obliged. Such was the force emanating from the god of sky and thunder that poor Semele caught fire from him and was consumed by the flames. In an instant a column of cool ivy sprang up to protect the unborn infant. Rescued by his father, Dionysus was sewn up in Zeus's divine thigh until ready to be born. At the appointed time, he was delivered by the god Hermes and given to the care of the nymphs on Mount Nysa where he grew up with nymphs and satyrs for companions and the perpetually drunk satyr Silenus for a tutor. His carefree days however were marred by the relentless persecution of Zeus's wife Hera, who could not tolerate any offspring of Zeus born out of wedlock.

---

[173] Though some dispute he ever was.

In most representations Dionysus is shown with the ivy – whether wreathed in it, trailing it, or twisted round his staff (the *thyrsus)*. His followers and worshippers wore the ivy in his honour. In the Euripides's play *The Bacchae* for instance, the prophet Teiresias and the former king Cadmus crown themselves with ivy in honour of Dionysus, urging the reigning Pentheus to do the same. 'Let me crown thine head with ivy/honour thou with us the god'.

Legends of Dionysus' adventures were many. He crossed the river Tigris reputedly on a tiger sent to him by his father Zeus, and the river Euphrates on a bridge woven from ivy and vine shoots (the bridge was still there when Pausanias visited it in the second century AD[174]). Having got as far as India he turned back and returned to Greece. 'In India,' wrote Theophrastus, 'ivy appears on the mountain called Meros whence, according to the tale, Dionysus came'. On the other hand, the inhabitants of Acharnai (Attica) claimed the ivy first appeared there and worshipped Dionysus and the ivy as one and the same god.[175]

The ivy was never carried into the temples dedicated to Hera, goddess of marriage and women. From that it had been inferred that sobriety was necessary for a happy marriage. The main reason, however, was its close link to Dionysus, resented by the vindictive Hera.

In historical times Alexander the Great, on reaching India, crowned himself and his army with the ivy in honour of the god to commemorate the event.

Once Dionysus, disguised as a prosperous young man, boarded a ship in Naxos. Out of sight of the land, the sailors decided to rob and kill him. They were about to lay their hands on him when a sweet smell of ambrosia spread through the ship, the oars and the mast became enveloped in the ivy, while they found themselves changed into dolphins. For this reason, the Greeks believed dolphins are friendly towards

---

[174] PGG.I p.481
[175] PGG.I p.92

humans, and would swim along ships, being but transformed sailors.

While on Mount Nysa, Dionysus invented the art of making wine. He left it equipped with a vine stock and a supply of wine, and went on to travel, accompanied by nymphs, satyrs, and an ever-increasing throng of female followers – the *Maenads*. With his merry, if wild, company he went to Thrace, Boeotia, Attica, and even beyond the Greek world. He stopped on the island of Naxos where he found Ariadne abandoned by Theseus.[176] His love for her was gentle and compassionate in marked contrast to the excesses of his companions the proverbially lecherous satyrs and his good friend the god Pan, who reputedly only joined him in order to boast he had slept with every nymph in his entourage. (Nymphs apparently are not immortal but live for a very long time.)

Resolved to teach mankind the process of wine-making, Dionysus chose a man from Attica called Icarius. Icarius was delighted with the result. Fired with enthusiasm he packed his belongings and a supply of wine, loaded them on a cart, and, accompanied by his daughter Erigone, and a dog called Maera, set out into the world to share the knowledge he had acquired under the divine tutelage. All went well, until he met some shepherds to whom he offered the wine. Unused to the intoxicating effect of an alcoholic drink, the shepherds thought he had tried to poison them and reacted with vengeance. They killed Icarius, quickly buried him under a pine tree, watched only by the dog, and fled. Erigone was away when it happened. On her return the dog led her to the spot where Icarius was buried. Overcome with grief and despair she hanged herself on the pine tree by Icarius' grave. The gods took care of the faithful dog – they immortalised it by setting its image in the sky, to be known as the Lesser Dog Star.

During village festivals, girls used to swing from trees in Erigone's memory, and libations were poured in her and Icarius' honour.

---

[176] Theseus, hero of Athens, killed the Minotaur and escaped from the Maze with the help of Ariadne whom he abandoned at Naxos.

This inauspicious beginning marked the god-given gift, which was to bring much cheer and enjoyment to mankind. After all, 'when wine is no more found, then Love is not, nor any joy beside is left to men', to quote a poet. To convey the empty vastness of the sea, Homer described it as 'the place where there is no wine-harvest'.

WINE-MAKING AND WINE

Wine is made from the fermented juice of the grape, *Vitis vinifera* and its varieties. Fermentation is brought about by the yeast, which occurs naturally on the surface of the fruit, converting the sugar contained in the grape into alcohol and gas (carbon dioxide) which normally escapes. The process had been known to mankind since time immemorial, probably even from the wild varieties before grapes were cultivated. The grape probably originated in Asia Minor, but the art of wine-making, well established by around 3,000 BC came to Greece either from Egypt or Crete. According to the ancient Greeks, however, it was the god Dionysus who taught mankind how to produce wine.

Methods of making wine varied little in antiquity. The harvested grapes were taken from the vineyards in baskets, put into vats or spread on a flat, grooved rock, and trampled, often to the sound of flutes. As the juice flowed out through the channels, it was collected in earthenware jars – the characteristically shaped amphorae, where it fermented. The amphorae were stored in cellars or caves at a relatively cool, constant temperature. To prevent evaporation, they were coated with pitch, the neck sealed with a piece of wood or cork and covered with fat. The handles on the jar were stamped with the name and place where the wine was made. These stamped jar handles were found in archaeological excavations in various parts of the world. Minoan Crete was probably the first country to elevate wine production from a domestic affair to a major economic export. The main wine-producing islands of Greece were

Rhodes, Cos, Lesbos, and Chios. The town of Arne (Lycia) was described by Homer as 'green with vineyards', and Phrygia was known as 'the vineyard country'.

A grape harvest was depicted by the goldsmith god Hephaestus on the shield of Achilles.[177] It showed a vineyard surrounded by a ditch, plants propped by poles, grapes being picked by boys and girls and collected in wicker baskets. A boy plucking a lyre sang a dirge to the dying year, while others romped around, skipped, and danced in time with the music.

The great hero Heracles was given the task of working in a vineyard belonging to a robber Syleus. Work, however, was not what he had in mind. Instead, he pulled up all the vines, which he used to make a fire to bake bread and roast meat. To add insult to injury he broke into Syleus's cellar and helped himself to his best wine, then invited him to share the meal. When Syleus furiously objected, Heracles killed him with a club.[178]

The soil of Phelloe (Achaia) was excellent for vine growing, reported Pausanias. He mentioned a bronze statue of a nanny goat in the market square of the city of Phlious. It was erected to propitiate the star called Nanny Goat which, when it rises, plays havoc with the cultivation of the vines.

Maroneira in Northern Greece had been famous for its wines since the days of Homer. Wines from Heraclea were considered the most fragrant. The celebrated Pramian wine (the drink of heroes) was described as neither sweet nor thick, but dry, rough, and very potent. It was not popular in Athens in spite of its reputed aphrodisiac properties. On the island of Thasos, Theophrastus was offered some wine in the town hall that he found of a 'wonderful, delightful' quality. Ever curious, he found it was flavoured with a lump of dough kneaded with honey 'so that the

---

[177] IRF18, 654-669 tr. Robert Fagles
[178] C. Kerenyi *The Heroes of the Greeks*, tr. H. L. Rose, Thames & Hudson 1997, p.196

wine gets the fragrance from itself and the sweetness from the honey'.

The wine of Erythrea tasted of brine, which Theophrastus found 'subtle and satisfying', so much so that if drank first there was no satisfaction in others. But then the Greeks did not refrain from adding sea water to wine to counteract the effects of intoxication. Those saline Greek wines found favour with the Romans.

As well as blending inferior wines, the Greeks added all kinds of herbs and seeds for flavour and fragrance and to prevent it turning to vinegar. The most common additives were anise seeds, rose petals, myrrh, honey, even chalk and powdered marble. Resinated wine, (i.e., flavoured with pine resin) served in present day Greece, was not mentioned before the Roman times. In Homer, we find that wine was served in a posset mixed with cheese, a barley 'meal' and/or honey. Many preferred their wine sweet, considering it less intoxicating than dry wine, though harder on digestion.

Chiron, the wise centaur and tutor to Greek heroes, had a reputation for making excellent wine. In a poem by Theocritus, two shepherds refer to it as they drink their wine, and wonder: 'Was it quite such a vintage as this/old Chiron poured for Heracles in Pholus' rocky cave?'

Dioscorides distinguished several kinds of wine: sweet, dry, black, hard, as well as the red and white varieties, and made several references to its medicinal uses. It was supposedly good for the stomach. Many dried herbal remedies were steeped or taken in wine. It was also widely used in the preparation of perfumes to enhance the scent, particularly that of the myrrh.

The Greeks remained ever grateful to Dionysus for the 'grief-assuaging wine' but did not forget the moral of the story of Icarius and drank their wine diluted. 'For,' as Odysseus famously reflected, 'wine is a crazy thing. It sets the wisest man singing and giggling like a girl; it leaves him to dance and it makes him blurt out what were better left unsaid.'[179] The norm was five parts of water to two parts of wine, half-half was considered very strong, and neat wine downright uncivilised. The centaurs, those savage half-man, half-horse creatures inhabiting Mount Pelion, had a reputation for drinking their wine undiluted, which in Greek eyes was appalling. Apparently, it was polite to add wine to water and not the other way round. Water was poured first into a special wine mixing bowl called the '*krater*'. Some of those bowls were huge – the silver one belonging to Achilles held six gallons, while that of the King of Pylos, Nestor, even bigger and of remarkable beauty, one which only he could lift. Once mixed with water, wine was drunk from a two-handled drinking cup called the '*kylix*'.

Most drinking cups and mixing bowls were decorated with the leaves and berries of the ivy of Dionysus. The poet Theocritus describes one such cup:

> *About its lip wind shoots of ivy, rich ivy*
> *with golden leaves spiralling around itself*
> *exulting in its yellow fruit.*
>> *The Idylls I, Thyrsis' Lament for Daphnis*[180]

It was commonly believed that ivy berries eaten before drinking counteracted the effects of wine. Those going for a night out often wreathed themselves with ivy. As one poet wrote:

> *Whilst with ivy twines I wreathe me*
> *and sing all the world beneath me*
> *others run to martial fights*
> *I to Bacchus's*[181] *delights;*
> *Fill the cup then, boy, for I*

---

[179] Homer, *The Odyssey*, Bk. IV, tr. E. V. Rieu, Book Club Assoc/Penguin 1973, p.227

[180] Tr. Anthony Holden, *Greek Pastoral Poetry*, Penguin 1974, p.46

[181] Roman; Greek – Dionysus

Drunk than dead had rather lie.

Anonymous – *The Pleasures of Wine*[182]

At banquets drinking began with a libation to Dionysus, by sprinkling a few drops of undiluted wine on the ground. After that, wine was mixed at the host's discretion, presumably getting stronger as the night wore on. There are many references to wine-mixing in Greek literature. To quote just one example from the Odyssey: 'Mulius mixed them a bowl of wine and they went round and served them all. They poured out their offerings to the blessed gods before drinking the mellow wine, and when they made their libations and drunk all they wanted they dispersed to their several homes for the night.'[183]

Attempts at moderation, however, are somewhat compromised by references in literature and the evidence provided by pottery artists, who depicted revellers in various stages of intoxication. Many herbal remedies and wreaths of a particular composition were recommended to counteract the effects of wine, pointing to the sad fact that the flesh is weak and succumbs to indulgence.

In Dionysus' sanctuary at Elis, where stood his statue by Praxiteles, every second year a miraculous event took place on his feast day – the basins filled with wine of their own accord. There was, however, a drawback to this miracle. Once taken outside the sanctuary the wine turned to water.[184]

---

[182] Tr. Thomas Stanley, *Greek Literature in Translation*, Penguin 1973, p.353
[183] *The Odyssey*, XVIII, tr. E. V. Rieu, Book Club Assoc./Penguin 1973, p.287
[184] According to Pliny

MEDICINAL PLANTS

Most medicines of the ancient world were derived from plants. Among the plants listed by ancient herbalists it is often difficult to distinguish between those used for their genuine healing properties and those ascribed with magic. To the ancient man all plants that brought a reaction in the human body were 'magic', it was just a question of whether they were beneficial or harmful, and this he found by trial and error. The ancient Greeks believed some herbs were discovered by the centaur Chiron, some by the god of medicine, Asclepius, some even by the hero Heracles who favoured drastic remedies.

Knowledge of the properties of herbs was not at all common, and those familiar with them were much respected. Homer, for instance, makes a special reference to Agamede, daughter of King Augeas, who 'knew every magic herb that grows in the wide world'. The indefatigable traveller Pausanias met a man in Cyprus 'who was skilled at sorting herbs for medicinal purposes', a skill rare enough to deserve a mention. The Egyptians, reputedly descended from Paean the physician to the immortal gods, possessed that knowledge, again mentioned by Homer: 'And in medical knowledge the Egyptian leaves the rest of the world behind. He is a true son of Paean the Healer'[185].

The properties of medicinal herbs were recorded in herbals. The earliest known herbal dates back to Sumer (third millennium BC) in the form of clay tablets inscribed with cuneiform writing, containing descriptions of pharmaceutical preparations, mostly herbal. The Sumerians used such plants as Cassia, Myrtle, Asafoetida, Thyme, Willow, Pear, Fig and Dates. Herbs were first pulverised, then infused in beer, wine, or oil.

Healing plants such as Cassia, Henbane, and Liquorice are mentioned in the Code of Hammurabi, the King of Babylonia (seventh century BC), who ordered records to be carved in stone. The Egyptians recorded their medical knowledge on the papyri. By the sixteenth century BC they already had a list of around nine hundred medical prescriptions containing plants.

Most of our knowledge of herbal remedies in antiquity relies on two important sources: Theophrastus and Dioscorides. Theophrastus listed curative plants in his work *History of Plants and Causes of Plants*. Dioscorides, physician serving in the army of Nero (first century AD), compiled about six hundred medicinal plants in his herbal *De Materia Medica*. It served as a medical textbook for nearly sixteen hundred years and formed the basis of most herbals of the Middle Ages.

Medicinal plants are effective in a number of ways, depending on how they are used, whether fresh, dry, or dissolved in liquids such as water, wine, or oil. Also, which part of the plant contains the required properties – whether leaf, root, seed, stem, or whole.

Most herbalists involved in the preparation of roots and herbs (the Greeks called them 'root-cutters' – *rhizotomoi*) tried to keep the knowledge of plant properties to themselves, transmitting it by word of mouth, protecting themselves by fanciful stories, and maintaining all kinds of rituals, such as magic spells and dream interpretations

---

[185] Homer, *The Odyssey*, IV, c.233.1, tr. E. V. Rieu, pub. Alan Lane 1973, p.70

(particularly practised in Asclepius's centre in Epidauros), to discourage the uninitiated.

What the plants were used for points to the hazards of life as it was then. There were remedies against plague which occurred all too often. The great number of poison antidotes implies the common presence of venomous snakes, rabid dogs, and poisonous insects. Some plants were believed to offer immunity against poison, though their efficacy must have been uncertain. Theophrastus noted with great interest that tolerance to poisoning could be built by voluntarily taking minute doses of poison and gradually increasing the dose. Apparently, slaves who were unhappy with their lot would eat just enough poison to induce sickness but not kill themselves, in order to scare their masters into conceding to their requests. Unfortunately, as Theophrastus wryly pointed out, not all knew the right dose and casualties did occur.

The most famous example is of the ruler of Pontus Mithridates (second century BC) who built an immunity to poison by regularly taking small doses, so that when an attempt was made on his life by poisoning his food it would have no effect on him.

Often a single plant was considered efficacious for a wide range of complaints, while some were even thought to cure practically all there was to cure, the so-called All-Heals. It might be obvious to us now in the light of modern knowledge that they could not possibly work, on the other hand, the ancient physicians were surprisingly right about some. Approximately half of the plants mentioned by Dioscorides are to be found in the present-day European pharmacopeia.

The Simples of Chiron

According to ancient myth there lived on Mount Pelion in Thessaly a tribe of savage, promiscuous, half-horse, half-man creatures – the Centaurs. They were the descendants of Ixion, King of Thessaly, who made love to a cloud shaped in the image of the goddess Hera, wife of Zeus. This extraordinary union came about when Ixion, invited to a banquet at Olympus, was struck by Hera's beauty and tried to seduce her. This was noticed by Zeus who quickly shaped a cloud to look like Hera. Ixion, too drunk to notice the difference, made love to it. The offspring of the union was Centaurus − half-man, half-horse, ancestor of the Centaurs. Zeus punished Ixion for his scandalous behaviour by having him bound to a fiery wheel that rolls ceaselessly across the sky.

The Centaurs had a bad reputation. Homer referred to them as wild beasts. They were quarrelsome, prone to excess and violence, easily intoxicated with wine which they habitually drunk undiluted, considered scandalous by the Greeks. They were involved in numerous hostile incidents. Probably the best known is their fight with the Lapithae, a mountain tribe in Thessaly, commemorated on the metopes of Athena's temple the Parthenon. It took place at the wedding of a ruler of Lapithae. Once the Centaurs got drunk, as was their habit, they attempted to carry off the bride and the women guests, provoking a fierce battle in which the Lapithae emerged victorious.

However, they did possess valuable knowledge of medicinal properties of herbs and their cultivation which, true to their belligerent nature, they were unwilling to share or divulge, with the notable exception of Chiron. Variously described as 'the civilised Centaur', the 'Learned One' or the 'Wisest of Beings', Chiron claimed a different parentage from the rest of the Centaurs. He was an offspring of the union of two early Greek deities − Philyra, daughter of Oceanus, the god of the river that encircles the earth, and Cronus the Titan. Their lovemaking was interrupted by the arrival on the scene of Cronus's wife. On seeing her, Cronus instantly transformed himself into a stallion and galloped away. The result was that Philyra gave birth to a half-horse, half-man creature − Chiron.

Chiron was famous for his skills in medicine, hunting, archery, music, and prophecy, all of which he taught willingly. His school at Mount

Pelion became famous as were his illustrious pupils – Asclepius, who was to become the god of medicine, Jason of the Golden Fleece fame, Achilles, the greatest hero of the Trojan War, Acteon, a Boeotian hero[186], Aeneas, the Trojan prince destined to become the founder of Rome, and many others. Even the gods Apollo and Artemis reputedly received instructions from him.

The great respect for Chiron's knowledge is evident in Homer. Eurypylus, wounded in battle, begs his comrade Patroclus to 'cut this shaft from my thigh ... and spread the soothing, healing salves across it, the powerful drugs they say you learned from Achilles and Chiron, the most humane of Centaurs taught your friend'[187].

Similar sentiments were expressed by the poet Pindar:

Deep counselling Cheiron
Nursed Jason inside his stone dwelling,
And Asklepios after him,
And taught him the use of medicine with gentle hands.[188]

Chiron's tragic end came through the violent temper of the Centaurs. They picked a fight with Heracles who came to visit him in his cave on Mount Pelion. In the ensuing skirmish, one of Heracles' poisoned arrows accidently struck Chiron wounding him gravely. Ironically, this great healer could not cure himself nor, being immortal, could he die. He continued to exist in constant pain with no hope of ever ending his agony, longing for death. According to some he managed to exchange his immortality with Prometheus (of the stolen fire fame), an unlikely story since Prometheus was immortal anyway. In the more likely version, Zeus gave in and allowed Chiron to die, but immortalised him anyway

---

[186] Acteon incurred the wrath of Artemis when he inadvertently saw her bathing in the nude. She changed him into a stag and set her dogs to tear him apart.
[187] IRF II,990-995, Penguin 1991, p.324,
[188] Pindar, *The Odes of Pindar*, *Nemean III* 52-55, pub. Penguin 1985, p.103, tr. C. M. Bowra

by placing his image among the stars. Chiron is represented as the Archer – Sagittarius, one of the signs of the Zodiac.

One of Chiron's most famous pupils was Asclepius who came to be venerated as the god of medicine, though not at first. (It is probable that the so-called gods of healing were in fact successful physicians whose expert skills and successes led them to be venerated). Heracles dismissed him as a 'root-digger and a wandering quack'. Homer referred to him merely as 'the blameless physician' whose sons Podaleirus and Machaon, also skilled in the art of healing, served in the Greek army in the Trojan war.[189] Machaon healed wounds caused by arrows and other weapons by washing, cutting, and sprinkling soothing powders of dried herbs. He was called to attend to Menelaus wounded in battle: 'Go quickly,' says Agamemnon to Talthybius the crier on seeing Menelaus' wound, 'And call Machaon, son of Asclepius, the great healer.' Machaon proceeded to suck the wound clean of blood, and sprinkle it with a balm, 'a medicine that Chiron gave his father'[190]. The people of Messenia (Peloponnese) believed Asclepius's sons were Messenian, and proudly pointed to Machaon's tomb and a sanctuary of his sons.[191]

Machaon's brother, Podaleirius, was the physician who healed the famous archer Philoctetes, the only man who dared to light Heracles' pyre. Heracles resolved to end his agony caused by a poisoned shirt given to him inadvertently by his wife by flinging himself on a pyre. In spite of his entreaties no one was willing to light it, until he bribed Philoctetes with his bow and poisoned arrows. On the way to Troy Philoctetes was bitten by a snake. The wound festered so much that his companion, unable to tolerate the stench, deserted him on the island of Lemnos. There he would have remained but for Odysseus, who, acting on the prophecy the war would not end without the arrows of Heracles, came to fetch him. He was accompanied by Podaleirius, who managed to

---

[189] IFTZ II, p.38
[190] IFTZ IV c. 220, pp. 62-63
[191] PGG II, p.109

restore Philoctetes to health.

In later accounts, Asclepius became deified as the son of Apollo and a mortal woman called Coronis. According to the story Coronis, while pregnant with Asclepius, tried to leave Apollo for a lover. When Apollo heard about it, he flew into a rage and killed her. Recovering his senses, he managed to tear the unborn infant from her lifeless body and give it into Chiron's care. Chiron taught him the art of healing at which Asclepius soon excelled, and even managed to bring a dead man back to life. That was more than the gods of the sky and the underworld, Zeus and Hades, were prepared to tolerate. Fearing that mortal men might find their way to immortality, annoyed by what they regarded as straying into the gods' prerogative, they decided to eliminate him. Zeus struck Asclepius with a thunderbolt.

On learning of his son's death, the outraged Apollo killed the Cyclops who provided Zeus with the fatal weapon. This infuriated Zeus further. He punished Apollo by making him work for one year as a hireling to a mortal. However, he relented enough to grant Apollo's wish to make his son immortal, by placing the image of Asclepius among the stars. Asclepius is known as the Serpent-holder, the serpent being the symbol of healing powers, renewal, and wisdom. Serpents were also believed to have powers of discovering medicinal herbs.

Asclepius's shrines and sanctuaries were scattered all over Greece. His main centre of worship was at Epidaurus, which he shared with his father Apollo, also venerated as a healer. Their cult centre reached its peak in the fourth century BC and continued to flourish well into Roman times. According to Pausanias, Asclepius was actually born at Epidaurus. His statue, described by him as half the size of the Olympian Zeus (which was huge), portrayed Asclepius in a sitting position, holding his symbolic staff in one hand, a serpent in the other and a dog lying by the side. The image was stamped on the coins of Epidaurus. His staff, with which he was frequently portrayed, was either entwined with two snakes and tipped with a pinecone, or crowned with laurel, the plant of Apollo, to stress their shared worship. The snakes, sacred to him, inhabited Epidaurus.

The sacred grove of Asclepius was surrounded by a boundary. No birth or death could take place within its enclosure. (The same rule applied to his father's sanctuary at Delos). Among many healing practices carried out at the centre was that of 'incubation', that is, sleeping within the temple precincts to find the cure from a dream. The priests of Asclepius, however, did not rely solely on the intercession of the god, and applied their medical skills as well.

To Asclepius, cocks were sacrificed (this, it will be remembered, was the last wish of Socrates). Votive stone slabs inscribed with names of patients healed by Asclepius, together with the details of their diseases and cure, were placed by the temple. Pausanias mentioned six when he was there in the second century AD.

Not only mortals were subject to sickness and injuries. The immortal gods also had their share of wounds, which they bore with little fortitude. Aphrodite when wounded ran to her mother to be consoled. Ares, struck in the belly during the Trojan war, instead of putting a brave face as befitting the god of war, crawled whimpering to father Zeus who thoroughly berated him. Hades was hit in the shoulder as he wandered among the dead. It was treated with a healing poultice. But, of course, all recovered as 'they were not born for death'.

The practice of healing the mortals brings us to a respected body of men and one in particular, to this day regarded as the Father of Medicine. This was Hippocrates, born around 460 BC on the island of Kos where stood another impressive sanctuary of Asclepius. He travelled widely throughout Greece before returning to Kos, gathering around him physicians, instructing them to keep records and exchange information, forming in this sense the first school of medicine. Hippocrates put great emphasis on careful observation of the symptoms of a disease, and study of the body and its functions, the operations carried out and the remedies applied, veering the art of healing away from the nebulous sphere of magic and putting it (within the limits of knowledge of his time) on an empirical basis. The data enabled the physicians to make a diagnosis and apply treatment. The collected works – the *Hippocratic Corpus* – is ascribed to him. In addition to surgical skills, a physician had to be thoroughly acquainted with the properties of medicinal plants. About two hundred-and-fifty different species are listed in the *Corpus*.

Hippocrates also laid down the ethics of conduct. Until recently medical graduates were required to swear the Hippocratic oath (parts of Hippocratic oath are still used by medical schools throughout the world). To quote:

> *'I swear by Apollo to reckon him who taught me this art equally dear to me as my parents ... I will give no deadly medicine to any one if asked nor suggest any such counsel ... Into whatever houses I enter, I will go into them for the benefit of the sick, and will abstain from every voluntary act of mischief ... Whatever ... I see or hear, in the life of men ... I will not divulge ...'* [192]

The appearance of a physician was also considered to be important. He was required to be 'clean in person, well dressed, and anointed with sweet smelling unguents that arouse no suspicion'.

Hippocrates reputedly gathered pupils under his favourite plane tree growing on Kos. It would be gratifying to think that something of the spirit of this great man under which he sat and taught might be still, as the ancients would have put it, *contained* in the plane tree that replaced it (the present tree is around five hundred years old, and in 1997 it measured forty-six feet).

Many aphorisms are ascribed to Hippocrates, such as: 'Where the love of man is, there is also the love of the art [of healing]'; 'where ever a doctor cannot do good, he must be kept from doing harm.' Towards the

---

[192] Quoted from *Classical Greece*, Great Ages of Man series, p. 103

end of his long life (he reputedly lived to almost a hundred), Hippocrates was left with few illusions: 'Life is short, and the art [of healing] long, the occasion fleeting, experience deceitful and judgment difficult'.

Once the influence of Greek learning had declined, the practice of medicine was plunged into a quagmire of ignorance, magic, and superstition, only to emerge from it in historically recent times. Reading through the *Hippocratic Corpus* one can only marvel at the systematic and scientific approach to medicine at such an early stage of human history and bewail its disappearance in the centuries that followed.

The enduring legacy of Hippocrates and his school continues to astonish and inspire. It is as well to be reminded of its quaint beginning – a bunch of healing herbs selected by the wise teacher, the civilised Centaur of Thessaly.

The handful of examples of medicinal plants used in antiquity listed here were chosen from ancient herbals for their historical and anecdotal interest.

THE ALL HEALS

In an age of ever-narrowing specialisation the idea of an 'all-heal' is treated with scepticism. But in the past, when it was possible to know all there was to know, a plant which, it was claimed, cured all or practically all, did not stretch credibility. The popularity of the 'All-Heals', or panaceas (so called after Panacea, the goddess of all-healing, daughter of Asclepius) were popularly believed to be richly endowed with curative powers, waxing and waning with fashion and with their advocates.

Theophrastus distinguished three kinds of All-Heals. That of the hero Heracles, friend and pupil of Chiron, was the Opopanax, borne out by its common name 'Hercules all-heal'. Resin extracted from the roots was applied to a wide range of ailments, from coughs to convulsions. An ointment was good for gout, eye diseases, and teeth cavities. Mixed with honey it was put on dry sores; drunk in sweet wine it was efficacious for stomach pains; mixed with pitch and made into plaster it was a remedy for bites of mad dogs. His other panacea was the <u>All-heal</u>.

Elecampane

This was the panacea of Chiron. Mixed with wine or made into plasters, it was good for venomous animals. According to myth, the elecampane sprang where the tears of Helen of Troy fell on the ground, hence its name derived from the corruption of 'Helen' or 'Elena'. An infusion made from the rhizome was used for bronchitis and digestive upsets.

Milkweed

When cutting the panacea of Asclepius, aptly called Asclepias (common name Milkweed), one was supposed not only to pray, which Theophrastus thought was not unreasonable, but offerings of fruit and cakes were also required, which he considered absurd. The 'all-heal of Asclepius' was described by him as having a stout root with a briny taste. It prevented long periods of sickness generally. For headaches it was made into an ointment by mixing it with olive oil and applied to the head. For running sores, it was sprinkled straight on the wound, for dry ones it was first soaked in wine. Taken internally in wine it was good for stomach aches. The scraped root was drunk for snake bites.

Vervain

One of the all-cures recommended by Hipppocrates was the Vervain, though whether this is the *Verbena officinalis* of the present day is not certain. The list of the alleged cures is very long and varied. An infusion made from dry leaves was diuretic, the poultice was good for inflammations and ulcers, mixed with fat it stopped pains of the womb, and taken neat it induced sweating. Sprinkled during banquets, it reputedly made the guests merry. Perhaps it was that belief that made it symbolic of enchantment.

Betony

One of the original medicinal herbs believed to have been discovered by Chiron and used by Asclepius was the Betony. A Latin treatise on the Betony included a prayer: 'Betony, you who were discovered first by Aesculapius[193] or by Chiron the Centaur, hear my prayer. I implore you, herb of strength, by him who ordered your creation and ordered that you should be useful for a multitude of remedies. Kindly help in making these seven and forty remedies.'[194]

It enjoyed a high reputation as a tonic, and also for its supposed magic properties, very successful against witchcraft and evil spirits.

Centaury

Regarded as an all-heal until classical times, the Centaury belonged to a flowering plant family called *Chironia* (now reclassified and put into the Gentian family) reflecting the belief that it was discovered by the centaur Chiron. According to legend the Centaury was applied to Chiron's fatal wound. This seems unlikely, as Chiron's wound never healed, and the Centaury's reputation would have suffered as the result.

Mugwort

This was the all-heal of the god Apollo whose cult was connected with his son's, the god of medicine, Asclepius. It might have been 'that certain herb' that Asclepius used to bring back to life, Glaucus, son of Minos, who drowned in a jar of honey and was revived by him.

The Mugwort's old name was *Artemisia mater herbarum* – the mother of all herbs, named after Artemisia, wife of Mausolus King of

---

[193] Greek Asclepius
[194] Quoted from *Englishman's Flora*, Latin treatise by Antonius Musa, ed. Howald & Sigerist *Corpus Medicorum Latinorum* p.346

Caria, who adopted it as an all-heal. It was used mainly for female disorders and was also supposed to alleviate fatigue and provide immunity to pain.

According to a different version, the Mugwort was named after the goddess Artemis, and used in the cases of 'precocious puberty'. Parents with difficult children must have found it a boon!

In another version, it was not Asclepius but the seer Polyeidus who was ordered to restore Glaucus to life. He tried without success, and so, to concentrate his mind, he was thrown into a tomb together with the dead boy. There, a serpent revealed to him a herb, believed to be the Mugwort, which revived Glaucus, and brought them both instant release.

Mistletoe

Dioscorides recommended the Mistletoe for a wide range of curative applications. Berries mixed with wax and resin were used for swellings. Mixed with Frankincense it was used for ulcers and malignant sores.

Sage

This common culinary herb was one of the most important medicinal herbs, regarded as the preserver of the human race no less: 'Salvia, salvatrix, naturae concilliatrix'. It was dedicated to the supreme ruler of the gods – Zeus himself. An infusion of dried leaves has disinfectant properties. It was applied for stomach upsets, nervous disorders, depression, dizziness, to name but a few. Leaves were burned as an insecticide.

Valerian

It enjoyed the reputation as an all-heal. It has calming, sedative properties, very effective as a nerve tonic and for a variety of other ailments, including snake bite.

Spurge

For a long time. Spurge was considered an all-heal. Fruit was used in miscarriages, diseases of the bladder and ear, and to strengthen the voice. The root was used in childbirth, women's diseases, and flatulence in beasts.

VULNERARIES

Plants used for healing wounds and sores were applied in a number of ways. Raw leaves of Mallow, Rue, Oregano, Clover or Fig were applied either directly or pounded and mixed with wine or roasted Flax seeds. Leaves of Pomegranate, Chaste Tree, and Rock Plant were boiled before application. Plasters were made from the leaves of Mullein, considered very efficacious for swollen or inflamed wounds, also from Lentils cooked in wine and oil and mixed with pounded Flax seed. Often the application of plasters was accompanied by incantations believed to assist the healing process. The bleeding wound of Odysseus, caused by a boar, was reputedly stopped in this way.

The Marsh Mallow, rich in emollient and soothing mucilage, hence good for inflammations and burns, was taken by those who underwent the gruesome ordeal, not uncommon in antiquity, of holding a piece of red-hot iron as proof of innocence. It is mentioned in the play *Antigone*[195] when the sentry pleads his innocence: 'All of us pleading ignorance ... ready to take up red-hot iron in our fists/go through fire, swear oaths to the gods ...' A person undergoing the ordeal wrapped his hand in a Marsh Mallow leaf before grasping the red-hot iron.

Mixed with sweet wine, it was recommended for coughs.

---

[195] Sophocles: *Antigone,* tr. Robert Fagles, Penguin p.72

Yarrow

The scientific name of the Yarrow (or Millefoil), *Achillea millefolium*, connects it to Achilles of the Trojan War fame, the greatest of Greek heroes, matched only by Heracles. (Alexander the Great believed himself to have descended from Achilles on his mother's side, and took time off to visit Troy, by that time an unimportant, backwater city, to honour his grave). Achilles used the Yarrow to treat the wounds of his comrades in the Trojan war, having learned the art of healing from Chiron, whose home, Thessaly, was his father's kingdom. Dioscorides wrote of the Yarrow: 'it keeps ye hurts of ulcers uninflamed smeared green or dry with acetum'. The root of the Yarrow has been identified as the 'bitter root' used in the treatment of a wounded warriors in battle, to dull the pain and to staunch bleeding.

For all his brilliant career and prowess in battle, Achilles was a morose character, haunted by the premonition of an early death, given to outbursts on a never less than grand scale, whether quarrelling over a captured woman or grieving the death of his friend Patroclus. This great warrior, whose feats in combat were legendary, not least for having slain the champion of the Trojans, Hector, is immortalized on a vase painting solicitously tending a wounded man.[196] The modest inflorescences of the Yarrow growing by a roadside bring to mind this moody giant of many passions – rage, petulance, grief, and solicitude.

Birthwort

A very old medicinal plant, its use recorded in ancient Egypt. A decoction of the fresh plant was recommended for wounds, ulcers, and snake bites. For the latter Theophrastus recommended the leaves to be mixed with sour wine, alternatively shredded leaves to be mixed with honey or olive oil. Taken internally, scraped into black, dry wine, it

---

[196] Inside a bowl by potter Sosias, c.500 BC, Berlin Stiflung Preussischer Kulturbesitz,Antikensammlung

induced sleep.

Loosestrife

Loosestrife is named after King Lysimachus who, according to legend, first used it 'to appease strife and unruliness' among oxen. A decoction of leaves was applied to wounds.

Plantain

The Greeks called it a 'lamb's tongue'. The leaves were used for wounds and sores. Alexander the Great reputedly considered it a wonderful cure for headache.

ADDITIONAL NOTES

Agrimony

Leaves crushed or infused were applied to wounds and sores.

Bear's Breech

Leaves macerated in cold water were made into dressings.

Bramble

Leaves for poultices.

Cuckoo Pint

Leaves for fractures.

Cyclamen or Sowbread

The root mixed with honey was made into dressings for suppurating boils.

Germander

Leaves pounded in oil were applied on wounds, spreading sores and fractures.

Male Fern

Leaves were applied to septic wounds, ulcers, and sores. Drunk, it was a remedy against tapeworms.

Marigold

Flower heads were made into poultices.

Mullein

Roots for wounds and for eye infections. Taken internally it was used for diarrhoea.

Roman Chamomile and Wild Chamomile

'Dioscorides saith, that with the fine pouder of Frankincense it healeth the wounds of the sinues' – quoted Gerard[197]

St. John's Wort

Soaked in olive oil, it encouraged the healing of wounds.

Thyme

Flowers heads were used for wounds, and taken internally for chronic stomach upsets.

---

[197] Gerard – *Generall Historie of Plantes*

PAIN KILLERS AND TRANQUILISING PLANTS

Tranquilising and pain-killing plants were widely used in antiquity with, presumably, variable effect. A remarkable account of one such plant, unfortunately unidentified, can be found in Homer. This was on the occasion of the visit of Odysseus's son, Telemachus, to Sparta, where he met Menelaus and Helen, reunited after the fall of Troy. When grief descended on the company assembled at the banquet as they reminisced about their fallen comrades, Helen decided to cheer them up. 'But now it entered Helen's mind to drop into the wine that they were drinking/an anodyne, mild magic of forgetfulness. Whoever drank this mixture in the wine bowl/would be incapable of tears that day – though he should lose mother and father both/or see, with his own eyes, a son or brother mauled by weapons of bronze at his own gate. The opiate of Zeus's daughter bore/this canny power. It had been supplied by Polydamna, mistress of Lord Thon, in Egypt, where the rich plantations grow/herbs of all kinds, maleficent and healthful; and no one else knows medicine as they do, Egyptian heirs of Paian, the healing god.'[198].

Theophrastus called that forgetfulness-causing drug 'Nepenthis'. He also noted that drugs grew better in some districts, Tyrrhenia in particular. It was known as 'Tyrrhenia rich in drugs', and the Tyrrhenians as people who make up drugs. Other places mentioned by him were Latium 'where they say Circe dwelt', and parts of Egypt. Most productive in Greece were Pelion in Thessaly, Telethrion in Euboea, Parnassus, Arcadia, and Laconia.

Mandrake

One of the most famous medicinal plants and one of the most important pain killers known in the ancient world, and used well into the Middle Ages, was the Mandrake. Its name *Mandrake* is traced to the Sumerian

---

[198] OFTZ IV, 219-226, p.71

'Nam-Tar' ('plague god plant') where it was used medicinally[199]. The root of the plant was boiled in wine and the draught given to the patient.[200] The dose was important – too much was believed to cause paralysis, madness, and even ultimately death.

Many strange stories and superstitions were associated with the Mandrake. Its forked root, resembling two legs, gave rise to the belief it was capable of striking dead anyone who tried to uproot it, and that it could run away shrieking when pulled out of the ground. To get round this problem, a starving dog was tied to the Mandrake and a piece of meat placed just outside its reach. As it strained after the meat, it pulled out the Mandrake, after which it was fully expected to drop dead. An illustration in one of the ancient herbals shows Dioscorides, or possibly Crateus, receiving the Mandrake from Herensis, the goddess of discovery, with a dead dog on the side, supposedly killed by an uprooted Mandrake.

Theophrastus did not mention the dog but described a complicated ceremony that accompanied the uprooting. First, a circle had to be drawn round it with a sword. The person doing the digging had to face due West. Having cut out the first root but before the second, the cutter should dance round the plant and say as many things as possible about the mysteries of love [sic!].

The root, once extracted, was cut into pieces like a radish, then hung on a string over a smoking fire. It was administered in wine and vinegar for pain. Given to lunatics it calmed them down.

Henbane

Used as a pain killer. Eaten cooked, it caused disturbance of the senses.

---

[199] From Lise Maniche *The Ancient Egyptian Herbal* pub. The British Museum Press 2006, p.125

[200] In the light of modern research, 'mandragora' on its own produces no such effect. Presumably it was mixed with other plants – henbane was one of the suggested species.

According to Dioscorides the juice and decoction of the seeds of *Hyoscyamus aureus* were the gentlest and the best.

SEDATIVES

Narcissus

Its narcotic properties (the name derived from '*narke*' – stupor) were known to the ancients. Homer referred to the Narcissus as the flower that delights with the scent and beauty, yet can produce stupor, madness and even death.

Opium Poppy

The sleep-inducing, narcotic properties of the Poppy were already recognised by the inhabitants of the Neolithic settlements in Switzerland, and certainly by the Sumerians. This powerful sedative plant contains opium, morphine, and narcotine, found in the latex of the green seed pod. Dioscorides gives a detailed account of the preparation of the opium. Drugs obtained from incised Poppy heads date from the commencement of the Christian era.

Belladonna

The bark of the root in wine deadened the pain by putting the patient to heavy sleep. Physicians used it before cutting or cauterising.

St. John's Wort

Sedative and anti-depressant.

TONICS

Tonics, taken in the form of infusions, were intended to restore, tone up and invigorate the body.

Balm

Crushed leaves of Balm give off a refreshing, pleasant smell of lemons. It was used in antiquity as a restorative, a cure for hypochondria, and in reducing the effects of fever. The oil derived from it was used for bites, stings, and wounds. The whole plant was particularly favoured by bees and planted next to beehives. It was sometimes called the 'bee-leaf', 'so-called because bees delight in this herb', wrote Dioscorides.

An infusion made of Balm leaves 'removed melancholy', drove away 'heaviness of heart', 'sharpened understanding' and improved memory.

Hog's Fennel

The root has warming properties, but the seeds and the juice are useless, warns Theophrastus.

Southernwood

A stimulating tonic and a remedy against intestinal worms.

Wormwood

A very popular gastric tonic, highly praised by Hippocrates who named it after the goddess Artemis. Also an excellent vermifuge.

Tansy

Made a stimulant tonic. The root preserved in honey was used in the treatment of gout.

Dandelion

A bitter tonic for stomach and urinary upsets.

Gentian

This was named after Gentius, King of Illyria (second century BC). Leaves steeped in wine were drunk as tonic. Dried, fermented rhizomes yielded a bitter tonic for stomach disorders. It was also an antidote against the bites of mad dogs.

Ground Ivy

Tonic, astringent, good against colds.

Hawthorn –Tonic

Sea daffodil – Tonic

Juniper

Apart from its use as tonic, it was good for stomach, thorax, coughs, and venomous beasts. The bark, steeped in water, was used to treat leprosy, but if swallowed would kill.

PLANTS WITH A WIDE RANGE OF APPLICATIONS

Rosemary

The oil obtained from the rosemary has antiseptic properties, greatly esteemed by the Greeks and Romans. It was also burned as incense.

Onion, Garlic

Both are mildly antiseptic.

Leek

Was good for warts, ring worm, and as a purgative.

Coriander

This aided digestion

Silphium

Now extinct. When it grew it was highly valued – excellent for a wide range of ailments (see also Vegetables).

Lavender

Yields oil, used for stomach and urinary upsets.

Myrrh

Its many medicinal uses much recommended by Dioscorides included sealing, drying, astringent.

Bitter Vetch

Recommended by Theophrastus for a number of complaints, particularly of teeth and gums.

Feverfew

For headaches

Lady's Mantle

Specially recommended for loss of appetite.

Wormwood

Expelled worms.

REMEDIES FOR FEMALE AILMENTS

Birthwort

Hippocrates used it for treating women during confinement (also *A.clematis*). Mixed with water, it was used to treat prolapse of the uterus.

Chaste Tree

Apart from being regarded as the 'preserver of chastity' (mentioned in connection with the feast of the 'Thesmophora'), a decoction of the leaves was a popular remedy for the disorders of the womb.

Cyclamen or Sowbread

They say that the root is a good charm for rapid delivery and a love potion', wrote Theophrastus. The root was burned, and its ashes mixed with wine were rolled into tiny balls. According to Dioscorides, if a pregnant woman stepped over the root, it would cause an abortion, but if tied round her body it would hasten delivery.

Dittany

Leaves mixed with water and made into draughts were taken for easy labour in childbirth. In addition, it was credited with the property of expelling foreign bodies such as arrow heads. If an animal, say, a goat or a sheep, was struck with an arrow, a handful of Dittany would help to expel it.

Mastic

The best Mastic came from the island of Chios. Dioscorides recommended it for diseases of the womb. He noted it was gently warming, binding, and mollifying.

Parsley

Given in wine for female disorders.

Vervain

Used to stimulate milk flow and regularise menstruation.

Sage

For increased fertility in women.

Poplar

Buds used in healing ointments.

Rosemary

Leaves were cooked in wine for a variety of ailments

Yellow Water Lily

The leaves stopped bleeding.

PURGATIVES

Among the purgatives the Hellebore stands out. The whole plant is poisonous, and the roots and the fruit are violently purgative. 'The plant should be dug up quickly', wrote Theophrastus, 'otherwise it would make one's head heavy'. The best way to dig it up was to eat some garlic first, followed by a draught of neat wine. The top of the root was useless and given to dogs to purge them.

The black root acted on the belly, the white by inducing vomiting.[201] Digging up the black Hellebore, wrote Theophrastus, required a

---

[201] PGG vol.I, p.506

particular ceremony. First a circle had to be drawn around the plant, then it was dug up facing East while praying and watching out for any eagles flying around at the same time. If an eagle was sighted in the vicinity, the person cutting the Hellebore would die within the year. Theophrastus, to his credit, dismissed those notions as irrelevant.

The Hellebore root reputedly retained its properties for thirty years. The white variety was given to sheep to purge them.

The plant was also called the 'Hellebore of Melampus', after the famous physician from Pelope in Peloponnesus, the first to draw attention to its medicinal properties. Melampus travelled to Egypt to study medicine where he noted the purgative properties of the Hellebore from its effect on goats. He was subsequently asked to cure the mad daughters of Proteus, King of Argos, who were convinced they had been changed into cows. He prescribed for them the milk of the goats previously fed on Hellebores, and they recovered. According to the story the grateful king offered him one of the daughters in marriage.

Hellebores grew abundantly on the island of Anticyra, and such was their reputation for curing mental disorders that the saying 'he ought to be sent to Anticyra' implied being of unstable mind and in need of treatment. The purgative properties of the Hellebores were quite drastic. In an incident quoted by Pausanias, large numbers of Hellebores were thrown into the river Plistus on the advice of Solon[202] during the siege of Athens by the Cirrhaeans. Once they had drunk the contaminated water, the Cirrheans became so ill with dysentery they had to abandon the siege.

Hellebores were also used as fumigants. Accompanied by incantations, they were used to purify sheep and horses also houses and temples, in the belief the smoke drove away evil spirits.

Included in the general term of 'Hellebores' is the diuretic White Hellebore (or False Helleborine) which causes vomiting. If grown in

---

[202] Athenian legislator and statesman 7-6 c. BC

vineyards it made the wine diuretic and people who drank it became emaciated.

Aloe

According to Dioscorides, the extracted juice of the Aloe was brought to Greece from India where it grew. He cautioned it should be yellow and not black. Considered a laxative.

Globularia

Violent in its purgative effect, known as 'Herba terrible'

Squirting Cucumber

The juice of the unripe fruit is violently purgative. It was used to treat rheumatism, paralysis, dropsy, shingles. Theophrastus recommended the root as a cure for white leprosy and mange in sheep.

ADDITIONAL NOTES

More plants with purgative properties

Betony – *Stachys officinalis*

Black Bryony – *Tamus communis,* roots

Buckthorn – *Rhamnus alaternus*, fruit

Common Fumitory – *Fumaria officinalis*, dried plant

Fig – *Ficus carica*, fruit

Laurestinus – *Iviburnum tinus*, berries

Mezereon – *Daphne mezereum*, bark

Mulberry – *Morus nigra*

Polypody – *Polypodium vulgare,* rhizome

Soapwort – *Saponaria officinalis*, rhizome

Spurge – *Euphorbia spp.*, sap

Violet – *Viola spp.*, root

White Bryony – *Bryonia cretica*, root

Yellow-Horned Poppy – *Glaucium flavum,* root.

REMEDIES FOR FALLING HAIR

Aloe – with wine; *Cabbage; Cress, Fir* – lotion; *Maidenhair Fern; Myrrh* – mixed with oils of Ladanum and Myrtle; *Water Lily* – mixed with pitch.

REMEDIES FOR SNAKE BITE, DOG BITE, AND OTHER VENOMOUS BEASTS

Asclepias or Milkweed

'Roots drunk in wine do help those bitten by poisonous beasts', wrote Dioscorides.

Asphodel

Drunk in wine causes vomiting, hence it was applied in cases of swallowed poison. Seeds and flowers in wine were considered particularly good against scorpions.

Bistort

Its contorted snake-like root was a remedy against snake bite, doubtless a case of sympathetic magic.

Bitumen Pea

For serpent bites.

Bugloss

A good remedy whether eaten, drunk, or hung round the neck for venomous beasts, particularly vipers. Chewed and spat into the mouth of the animal would kill it.

Carrot

Seeds when drunk were especially good for bites of venomous beasts. If drank before being bitten would make a person immune to snake bites.

Cress

Recommended for bites

Corn Cockle

For scorpion bites.

Chaste Tree

Fruit taken internally was good for serpents' bites. Leaves drove away venomous animals.

Eryngo

Roots

Fennel

Juice good for dog bites, scorpion stings, and poisoned arrows.

Germander

A decoction good for venomous animals. Strewn under a mattress drove away snakes.

Gold Flower

Root steeped in wine was good against venomous beasts.

Juniper Berries

Leopard's Bane

The root resembles a scorpion; hence it was supposed to be good for scorpion bites – a case of sympathetic magic. The plant was also supposed to kill all kinds of wild beasts, such as panthers and wolves. According to Theophrastus it was fatal to sheep, oxen, and other beasts of burden.

Larkspur

Seeds in wine were used for scorpion bites. The whole plant if placed near the scorpions weakened and paralysed them.

Lords & Ladies

Hands rubbed with the root will keep vipers away.

Leontice

Pounded root good against the bite of shrew mice.

Manna Ash

Effective remedy.

Mint

Mixed with salt it was good for dog bites. The species *M. longolifolia* was particularly efficacious for serpent bites.

Mugwort

Worn on feet drove away venomous animals and devils.

Roman Nettle

For dog bites

Oleander

For ulcers and snake bites. Additionally, it has the power 'destructive of dogs and asses and of mules and of most four-footed creatures,' writes Dioscorides.

Rue

Dioscorides had numerous uses for this plant. Both this species and the fringed rue, *R. chalepensis,* were used as counter-poison and against snake bites.

Tassel Hyacinth

Ointments made for dog bites and bruises.

Winter Marjoram

With wine good against venomous animals. Strewn under a mattress it drove away serpents.

APHRODISIACS

The ascribed aphrodisiac properties of some plants made them symbolic of fertility.

Orchids

The reputation of Orchids as powerful aphrodisiacs was based on the resemblance of the tubers to testicles. It was further enhanced by the belief that tubers were the food of the sexually excitable Satyrs, companions of Dionysus.

Orchids were believed to have arisen from the drops of Satyrs' semen that fell on the ground. In another legend, their origin was traced to a youth called Orchis, offspring of a union of a satyr and a nymph. Once, at a feast of Dionysus, Orchis was seized with a violent sexual desire and attempted to rape one of Dionysus's priestesses. The incensed Maenads tore him to pieces. His father begged the gods to restore him to life, but with no success. All they were willing to do was to transform Orchis into the plant that bears his name.

The tuber of the Orchid was said to 'stir up courage in conjunction' to use an old-fashioned phrase. It would provoke sexual desire if held in hand, but even more if drunk in wine. Dioscorides mentioned another property of the tubers, if a man should eat the bigger tuber of the *Orchis rubra* before intercourse he would beget boys. The smaller, eaten by a woman, would result in a girl. Women of Thessaly offered a fresh tuber in goats' milk to 'provoke venerie', while a dry tuber was said to suppress it.

Carrot

This popular culinary vegetable was associated with love affairs. Orpheus maintained the Carrot wins love and excites passion, confirmed hundreds of years later by Dioscorides who stated that the Carrot 'cooperates to conception and provokes conjunction'.

Salad Plants

These were also endowed with such powers. The *Cress* supposedly incited copulation (but was bad for stomach, 'troubling the belly and lessening the spleen'), as did the *Rocket* and seeds of the *Parsley*, considered an abortive as well. The *Mint*, if taken before an intercourse helped conception.

The *Dragon Arum*, when drunk in wine stirred up 'the vehement desire to conjunction', as did the upper root of the *Gladiolus*, while the *Cyclamen* excited 'voluptuous desire'.

Mandrake

Some plants were made into love potions, of which the Mandrake was the most powerful. The women of Thessaly made them from the *Plantain*.

Enchanter's Night Shade

The fruit of the Enchanter's Night Shade, covered with hooked spikes and clinging to passers-by, was compared to the enchantments of the witch Circe. Hence the plant has been named after her. Circe was reputed to have used it to induce temptations to affairs of the heart.

CONTRACEPTIVES AND REPRESSANTS

The listed plants represent the *belief* in their efficacy. Whether they brought about the required results remains unproven.

Chaste Tree

The most widely used was the Chaste Tree, particularly in the celebrations of the Thesmophora in honour of the goddesses Demeter and Persephone. The women taking part slept on them believing that this would cool sexual urges and prevent immodest dreams. Dioscorides mentions it in his Herball: 'It is called Agnus, because in the sacrifices of Ceres [i.e., Demeter] the chast matrons did use it for strawing under them'.

Water Lily

A drink made from roots and seeds of the Water Lily allayed lecherous dreams. The root was thought to suppress sexual excitement so effectively it was nicknamed 'the destroyer of pleasure'.

Hemlock

A decoction of leaves and fruit of hemlock spread on the testicles 'helps wanton dreamers and seed shedders', while drinking an infusion of the root of asphodel will make men lose their sexual appetite.

Pepper

The fruit pods of pepper hindered conception, and the flower of the Cabbage was applied internally after childbirth.

Among others mentioned were the Asparagus, which made one barren and 'unfit for generation' according to Discorides, as would anointing with Oil of Cedar before intercourse, or leaves of the Willow drunk in water.

ADDITIONAL NOTES

More plants with ascribed aphrodisiac properties:

Basil – *Ocimum basilicum*

Chicory – *Cichorium intybus*

Fenugreek – *Trigonella foenum-graecum*

Henbane – *Hyoscamus niger*

Hogweed – *Heracleum spondylium*

Lettuce – *Lectuca sativa*

Navelwort – *Umbilicus rupestris*

Savoury - *Satureia hortensis*

Poppy – *Papaver somniferum*

Sea Holly – *Eryngium maritumum*, root.

MAGIC, POISONS, DRUGS

The Herbal of Medea – Plants Used in Magic
In such a night
Medea gather'd the enchanted herbs
That did renew old Aeson...

Shakespeare, *The Merchant of Venice* – Jessica

Whereas in present times the properties of plants continue to be analysed scientifically, in the past the ancient man ascribed them to the mysterious forces of nature. To influence them required occult or ritualistic methods. No wonder, therefore, that elaborate ceremonies and rituals to propitiate them grew around the plants capable of bringing about change in the body, the mind, and events. It took a great man like Theophrastus to dismiss some of the practices, but he was exceptional. 'What is said of amulets and charms,' he wrote, 'is somewhat foolish and incredible'. Yet superstitions remained unchallenged, and continued for centuries, to some extent to the present day. We still tend to cherish our charms.

A distinction should be made between the benevolent magic power to heal contained in medicinal plants, and the 'magic' released in the form of secret, supernatural forces springing either from the basest of motives, such as greed, revenge and destruction, or from the well-intentioned ones to drive away evil and bring about the fulfilment of dreams.

A theme recurring throughout mythologies is that of a magic herb or a wand capable of opening all locks, finding hidden treasure, or enabling the possessor not only to travel to the underworld, but to return from it, and even confer immortality.

One such herb capable of conferring immortality features in the oldest written epic. The Sumerian hero Gilgamesh managed to find it against great odds, only to lose it in a moment of carelessness. Although not achieving the kind of immortality he sought, Gilgamesh did gain immortality as the Greeks understood it, that is, living forever in human memory. Indeed, his name and deeds endured for more than five thousand years, although not thanks to a plant but a pen[203].

The malevolent kind of magic in the Greek world was practised by Medea, a powerful sorceress renowned for her skills. This dark, brooding daughter of Aetes, King of Colchis, was the niece of the witch Circe, and a priestess in the service of Hecate, the supreme deity of witches and magic arts. Medea would probably have remained in Colchis practising her arts, serving those two deities, were it not for a moment of fatal weakness. She fell deeply and passionately in love with Jason, the leader of the Argonauts, who had arrived in the *Argo* at Colchis to fetch the Golden Fleece. As soon as her eyes fell on Jason, 'Eros flew one of his arrows at her heart'.

King Aetes granted the Argonauts their request on impossible conditions, hoping in this way to be rid of them. Before he would hand over the Fleece, he told them, Jason was to yoke two fire-breathing, brazen-footed bulls, plough the field of Ares and sow it with serpents' teeth. But Aetes did not reckon with his daughter. She grasped at the chance and offered to help the Argonauts, on condition that Jason would swear by all the gods to marry her and keep faith with her for ever. Who can blame Jason for taking the oath? Having got so far through perilous seas and many adventures, the prospect of returning home empty-handed

---

[203] Strictly speaking a pointed reed marking a clay tablet

was not to be contemplated. Death would have been preferable. Medea's offer came at the most opportune moment. So, Jason swore by all the gods to comply with her wish.

Medea gave Jason a potion to protect him from the fiery bulls, said to contain an extract from a two-stalked saffron crocus that had sprung from the blood of the tortured Prometheus. Jason proceeded to carry out the task her father had set. Once accomplished, Jason presented himself to King Aetes who now revealed his true intentions. Not only did he refuse to part with the Golden Fleece, but even threatened to burn the ship and kill the crew if they continued to press their claim.

In response, Medea took Jason to the grove where the Golden Fleece hung on a tree guarded by a dragon who never slept. She mixed a powerful sleeping potion and sprinkled it in the dragon's eyes with instant effect. Together they took down the Golden Fleece, made their way to the *Argo*, and sailed away. On learning of their escape, Aetes, seized with fury, set sail in pursuit. As his ship approached the *Argo,* Medea killed her half-brother who had come with her, throwing the dismembered body piece by piece into the sea. This obliged the Colchians to stop and collect the pieces in order to give the body a proper burial, delaying them long enough for the Argonauts to make their escape.

Successful as the outcome was, the Argonauts' reaction to the gruesome murder was one of horror and revulsion, none more so than Jason's, as the realisation of the kind of person to whom he had pledged his faith hit him. But there was no turning back. The Argonauts insisted on purification of their crime, ordered by the oracular oak beam from Dodona fitted to the prow of the *Argo*. They stopped at the island of Aeaea where Jason and Medea were reluctantly purified by her aunt, Circe.

Jason kept his promise and married Medea in Corcyra (Corfu). After many adventures the *Argo* sailed to Iolcus, Jason's homeland, where he had a rightful claim to kingship. In his absence, his half-uncle Pelias had usurped the throne, eliminating both his parents and his younger brother.

Indeed, Jason had been sent out on an errand to fetch the Golden Fleece in order to keep him out of the way. The Argonauts swore revenge, but it was Medea who took the initiative. Dressed as a priestess of Hera, she went to the king's palace, where she was received by Pelias and his daughters. First, she managed to impress them with her magic arts, then claimed she could make people regain their youth, and could prove it. A ceremony was staged in which she pretended to rejuvenate an old ram by changing it into a lamb. While the fascinated daughters of Pelias were watching, she hacked the old ram into pieces, plunged them into a cauldron of boiling water, sprinkled powders, all the while muttering spells and incantations. Out popped a frisky lamb she had contrived to hide without anyone noticing. The daughters were so impressed they persuaded Pelias who was becoming old and infirm, to undergo the same treatment. He consented. The daughters cut him into pieces, put them into the cauldron of boiling water, sprinkled powders, recited incantations but, to their horror, the pieces failed to rise in any recognisable form. At that point, Medea gave a prearranged signal for the Argonauts to storm the city.

Jason did not stay long at Iolcus. He resigned his throne, either from fear of the vengeance of Pelias's son, or by accepting the adverse verdict of the Iolcan council. He and Medea went to Corinth where, through Medea's family connections, he became king and ruled for ten years. In that time Medea bore him two sons. As he grew older, Medea reputedly restored him with doses of a decoction made up from an aged deer and the head of a crow that had outlived nine generations.

They were not popular, people were terrified of Medea and her powers. Eventually even Jason had had enough. He courted Glauce, daughter of the Corinthian king Creon. Medea, pretending to accept the role of an abandoned wife, sent the young bride a wedding garment. As soon as Glauce put it on it burst into flames, consuming the bride, most of the wedding guests, and setting fire to the palace. Jason miraculously escaped. In a final act of spite, Medea murdered both their sons before

Jason could rescue them and fled, reputedly in a chariot drawn by winged dragons. A memorial to the children of Medea was seen by Pausanias in Corinth.

Jason ended his days a broken man, wandering homeless from city to city. Eventually he returned to Corinth where his old ship the *Argo* lay rotting on the beach. He continued to stay by the ship that took him to fame. Eventually, he took his own life by hanging himself from the prow, though some said he was crushed to death by the falling timber.

Of Medea, news came from time to time. She turned up in Athens where she married the king of Athens, but was banished after attempting to poison his son, Theseus, with the herb Aconite dissolved in wine. She went back to Colchis, to the island where her brother was buried, by that time overrun by snakes. Using her magic arts, she tried to confine them to his tomb. Of her death, nothing is known. According to some, like a true witch, she never died but became immortal and went to live with Achilles in the Elysian Fields.

The most dreaded divinity was Hecate, respected even by Zeus himself. Zeus kept his distance, never denying her the power to bestow or withhold from the mortals any desired gift. Hecate was represented with three heads and three bodies – of lion, dog, and mare – signifying her influence in heaven, earth, and the underworld. A triple statue of Hecate was particularly venerated on the island of Aigina, where her mystery was celebrated once a year.

All the magic arts were at Hecate's disposal. She knew the properties of every herb that grew on earth and used them for her dark purposes. She would emerge from her residence in the underworld to visit the earth at night, accompanied by a retinue of hellhounds and ghosts. Her favourite haunts were cemeteries, crossroads, and places where gruesome crimes had been committed. It was wise to appease her. People sacrificed black puppies to her, and left offerings of eggs and fish at the crossroads.

For I sing
to Hecate below,
in whose path even the dogs tremble
as she comes and goes across the graves
of the dead, over their dark blood.

Hail, dread Hecate! Be with me to the end
Give my drugs the power of Circe's
Or Medea's, or those of the golden-haired Perimede[204]

Compared to Hecate, the witch Circe dwelling on the island of Aeaea seems almost playful. It was she who turned the companions of Odysseus into swine when they beached their ship on her island. She met them as they wandered inland to explore the place, invited them to a feast and served them wine laced with magic potion, which brought about their transformation. Odysseus, who had stayed behind, managed to escape the same fate, thanks to the god Hermes whom he met while looking for them. Hermes gave him a magic herb called 'Moly', rendering him immune to Circe's magic.

Countless efforts were made to identify this plant, but it remained something of a mystery. It was described as having a white, scented flower, a black root, was difficult to dig up, and could only be recognised by the gods. Many tried to identify it among the living flora. The Wild Rue was one choice. Another which fitted the description was the Wild Cyclamen, having whitish petals, a dark bulb and being difficult to find. Or it could have been the Mullein. Dioscorides identified it as a species of Wild Garlic[205]. He wrote: 'the herb "moly" being cut up by ye root & borne about ye body is good against poisonings and bewitchings'. Theophrastus was equally sure of its identity. '"Moly" of Homer's fame,

---

[204] Theocritus, *The Idylls II, The Sorceress*, tr. Anthony Holden, Greek Pastoral Poetry, Penguin, p.52
Perimede – a woman skilled in the knowledge of herbs and enchantments
[205] *Alium nigrum* or *Alium dioscorides*

grows best in Pheneos and Mount Kyllene. It has a root like onion, leaf like a squill and is used against spells and magic arts. Unlike that of Homer is not difficult to dig up'.

MEDEA'S DRASTIC MEASURES – POISONS

Crowfoot

The 'Ilyrian crowfoot' mentioned by Pliny could refer to Crowfoot, or to the Field Buttercup[206] which is poisonous but 'when drunk causes man to see strange sights and would not cease laughing', hence its reputation of killing by laughter. In fact, it caused convulsions which made it appear as if the victim had died laughing. 'The island of Sardinia,' wrote Pausanias, 'is free from poisonous herbs but one which looks like a celery. Those who eat it, die laughing.'[207] He could have been writing about the Hellebore whose appearance might be confused with the Celery.

Golden Thistle

The root of the Golden Thistle was reputed to cause madness. Theophrastus quoted an example of a sculptor, Panedeios, who ate it and went mad while working on a temple. Roots growing near mines in Thrace were sweet in taste. In large amounts the root caused death, apparently very easy, like falling asleep.

Hellebore

The Hellebore is a powerful poison and a drastic purgative. Theophrastus noted that the poison becomes ineffective to those accustomed to it. He mentioned a druggist, Thrasyas, 'very cunning in the use of herbs', who could eat a Hellebore without ill effects, also a shepherd, who came up to

---

[206] (*Ranunculus acris*)
[207] PGG I, p.450

a vendor of drugs, ate a bundle of poisonous plants without being in any way affected, and destroyed the vendor's reputation.

White Hellebore was used to poison arrows.

Hemlock

This very poisonous plant kills even in small doses. Most of the poison is contained in the seeds (they lose some of their potency when dried). The citizens of Athens sentenced to death were given a cup of hemlock to drink. In the most famous case, it was given to the philosopher Socrates, sentenced to death for allegedly corrupting the youth of the day. His last moments and the effect the plant had on the human body were described in detail by Plato.[208]

Meadow Saffron

The Meadow Saffron had a reputation as a violent poison. Theophrastus wrote that slaves knew the cure for it. When greatly provoked by their masters they would take it, then, having frightened their masters sufficiently, cure themselves with an antidote. It did not always work, and killed by choking, like mushrooms.

Monkshood

One of the most poisonous European plants, the Monkshood, had been rubbed on arrows and spears since the earliest times and, like hemlock, was applied in capital punishment. Pliny called it the 'plant arsenic'. Any contact with it was dangerous, causing skin disorders.

Monkshood was also known as 'Hecateis', after Hecate, who reputedly raised it from the spittle of the dog Cerberus, guardian of the entrance to the underworld. Used both by her and Medea it acquired a bad reputation. It was credited with many malignant influences, such as causing fever in Corinth during Medea's sojourn there.

---

[208] Plato, *Phaedo* 117A -118, Penguin 1987, pp.182-183

Put to such evil uses, this pretty plant became the symbol of corruption, poison, and death.

Thorn Apple

Both the leaves and the seeds are toxic, causing madness. According to Theophrastus '3/20th of one ounce makes a man think he's a fine fellow, twice the dose causes delusions and makes him go mad, three times the dose makes him permanently insane, four times the dose, with the juice of the centaury for good measure, causes death.'

Wolf's Bane

The root of the Wolf's Bane is very poisonous, causing instant, painless death. Theophrastus noted the time between picking and administering it was crucial, as the time it took to kill was equal to the time elapsed from the moment it was picked. Thus, death could be delayed for several months and even a year or two. The longer the delay the more painful the death. There was no known cure. Dioscorides added that wild beasts, notably wolves, were killed by it when mixed with food – hence its name. Wolf's Bane reputedly grew best in Heraclea in Pontus.

ANTIDOTES TO MEDEA'S MINISTRATIONS – POISON REMEDIES

Ash

An infusion of ash leaves in wine was believed to be a powerful poison antidote according to Pliny and Dioscorides.

Buckthorn

The Buckthorn, a powerful purgative, was an effective poison antidote. According to Dioscorides: 'If any take up Rhamnus, ye moone decreasing and bear it, it is good against poisons and naughty men, it is good against beasts to bear it and put about ships and good against headaches and against devils and their assaults."[209]

Rue

It reputedly neutralised the poison if large amounts were eaten prior to ingesting. Rue was said to be the chief ingredient of the anti-poison potion of the emperor Mithridates (136-68 BC) who feared assassination by poison. He managed to build up remarkable immunity by regularly taking small doses of the poison.

Smilax

Leaves and fruit counteracted the effects of poison before and after swallowing. Given to a new-born child conferred immunity.

Citron

Citron mixed with wine caused vomiting, thus expelling the poison which has been swallowed.

ADDITIONAL NOTES

POISONS

Cyclamen – Cyclamen purpurascens

Very toxic plant, powerful purgative, used to poison arrows.

---

[209] All quotations from: Dioscorides: *De Materia Medica* tr. John Goodyear in 1655, Hafner Publishing Co.

Cowbane – Cicuta virosa

Very poisonous, contains substances causing violent cramps and affecting the brain.

Death Cap – Amanita phalloides

The best known and arguably the most poisonous of all fungi. Fungus poisonings were far from rare, whether by accident or design.

Leopard's Bane – Doronicum caucasicum

Believed to kill wild animals (hence the name) as well as domesticated ones, even on the same day, if the root or a leaf is put on their genitals.

Mezereon – Daphne cnidum

Very poisonous, called the 'destroyer of life'. Four berries were reputedly enough to kill a pig, eight a human being.

Oleander – Nereum oleander

Poisonous, but if taken in wine made one gentle and cheerful.

Wild Larkspur – Consolida regalis

Highly toxic, producing symptoms similar to that of Monkshood.

Deadly Nightshade – Atropa belladonna

Poisonous and narcotic.

Yew – Taxus baccata

The whole plant is poisonous with the exception of the red skin covering the berries.

PLANTS OF CHARMS AND MAGIC

Name Lost for Ever

The oldest 'magic' plant in history, capable of restoring youth, physical fitness, even immortality, is mentioned in the great saga of the Sumerian hero, Gilgamesh. His fear of death set him on a quest to find this plant.

> *There is a plant that [looks] like a box-thorn*
> *it has prickles like a dog rose and will [prick one who plucks it].*
> *But if you possess this plant,*
> *[you'll be again as you were in your youth]*[210]

He did manage to find it against tremendous odds, only to lose it to a serpent.

Mistletoe

Great many plants were thought to be capable of containing magic and widely used. The Mistletoe, also referred to as the 'golden bough', was arguably the most powerful magic plant of antiquity, to the point of allowing the bearer an entry to the underworld[211]. Aenas, the Trojan leader, armed himself with the Mistletoe while descending to the underworld to consult his father's spirit. The boatman Charon, on seeing it, raised no objections and ferried him across the Styx. The plant gave Aenas the power to return to the upper world.

The flame-coloured, golden leaves of the Mistletoe were seen as manifestations of the fire of the sun, believed to be residing in the tree on which it grew. The tree, particularly the oak, was thought to contain fire within it. Its twigs were used to start a fire by rubbing them together, thus bringing its latent fire out into the open. Hence, the Mistletoe was

---

[210] *The Epic of Gilgamesh*, Tablet XI, tr. Andrew George
[211] Virgil *The Aeneid*, VI, 200-215, tr. Robert Fitzgerald, pub. Penguin Books 1983, p.164,

thought to be the manifestation of that powerful element containing equally powerful magic properties. Added to it was the mystery of its life history, appearing, as it were, from nowhere without obvious roots, which was interpreted as a visible sign of being particularly favoured by the gods.

Peony

The Peony, used medicinally since early days, was named after Paean, the physician to the immortal gods, was also endowed with magic properties. Dioscorides wrote: 'The herb Peony is plucked up in ye heat of ye dog days before the rising of the sun and it is hanged about one & is good against poisons & bewitchings & fears & devils & their assaults & against fever that comes with shivering, whether by night or by day, or a quartan'. Devils could not congregate where it grew, as it drove them away. The most potent part against witchcraft were the seeds. The root was made up into amulets.

Theophrastus described the ceremony of digging up the root of the Peony. It should be dug up at night. If dug up during the day, and the digger happened to be seen by a woodpecker, he would risk losing his sight. Cutting only the root would result in 'prolapsus ani'. Theophrastus' comment: 'This is irrelevant'.

The root was given to women not cleansed after childbirth, to help abdominal pains. Black seeds were good for suffocations that 'come of nightmares', as well as from other causes.

Willow

The Willow was associated with lunar magic. The moon, believed to have profound influence on human affairs and all living things, played an important role in magic and religious rites. Closely bound with the phases of the moon were the fertility rites performed in the distant past in honour of nature goddesses during which a human male victim was tied to a sacred tree with Willow thongs supposedly rich in magic powers, and flogged until he ejaculated, fertilizing the earth with semen and blood.

The waxing moon represented a young virgin. The young virgin huntress Apollo's sister, the goddess Artemis, associated with woodlands and animal life, bore a silver bow of the new moon on her head. The full moon represented a fertile, mature woman, the waning moon a crone.

The moon was also considered to be the ruler of all waters. Willows favour moist localities and often grow by waters' edge; hence, a connection was established between the Willow and the magic forces emanating from the moon. The magic powers contained in the Willow were further confirmed by its medicinal properties. It was used to treat rheumatism thought to be caused by witchcraft, administered by the magic contained in the Willow.

Bay or Laurel

Apart from its other associations, the Bay or Laurel was a magic plant against bad luck. The saying 'I carry a Laurel', spelled 'I have no fear of magic or sorcery'. Branches of Bay were hung in cases of severe illness, to avert death and evil spirits, and to place the person under the special protection of Apollo to whom the Bay was sacred. 'The superstitious,' commented Theophrastus wryly, 'kept bay leaves in their mouths all day to guard them from misfortune'.

Crown Daisy

If gathered during the waxing moon, it was a force to be reckoned with against devils, spells, fears, and poisons. The root if chewed should be spat out. Also, a medicinal plant, good for aches, pains, and as a laxative.

If picked before sunrise, wrote Dioscorides, the Crown Daisy 'bound to ye body & hung on the neck averts witches and all enchantment'.

Gold Flower

Crowning oneself with the gold flower was believed to bring fame. So would sprinkling with an unguent from a vessel made of unfired gold. The root, steeped in wine, was good against venomous beasts.

Hazel

An important protector against witchcraft. Branches were made into magic rods. Hermes in particular had one, as had the goddess Athena, and even the witch goddess Circe.

Mugwort

Worn on the body, this 'Herb Artemisia' reputedly 'dissolved' weariness. Worn on the feet it drove away venomous animals and devils.

Christ's Thorn or Paliurus

It is said that branches being laid in gates and windows do drive away the enchantments of witches.

Squill

Planted before the entrance door of a house would 'ward off mischief which threatens it'. It was hung in houses in the New Year fertility rites.

Vervain

This was endowed with magic attributes. It was the 'Sacra Herba' – 'because it is fit to use in ye expiations to serve for amulets'[212]. The names given it– Cerealis, Demetria, Persephonium –suggests its use in the Eleusinian Mysteries. It was also known as 'Tears of Hera' and 'Hermes' Blood'.

---

[212] A 'Sacred Herb' *Hierabotane,* is mentioned by Dioscorides

ADDITIONAL NOTES

Betony – Stachys officinalis

The original herb of magic, discovered by Chiron, used by Asclepius.

Tormentill – Potentilla erecta

Effective against evil spirits.

Silphium – Ferula narthex

Believed to contain magic properties

Rue – Ruta graveolens

Effective (on its own and with wild parsley) against evil spirits and witchcraft.

Leek – Allium ampeloprasum

Contained magic against lightning.

Parsley – Petroselinum crispum

Warded off evil spirits.

Juniper – Juniperus communis

Burning berries banished evil influences.

Garlic Allium sativum

A charm against the evil eye.

Chaste Tree –_Vitex agnus castus

Worn as charm against poison. Would also cool sexual urges.

Blessed Thistle – Cnidus benedictus

A protective plant of magic and an all-heal.

Bittersweet – Solanum dulcimara

Effective in counteracting evil spells cast by witches.

Centaury - Centaurium umbellatum

Discovered by Chiron, used against evil spirits and witches.

Ash – Fraxinus excelsior

The tree was endowed with the magical powers of scaring away serpents.

PLANTS AFFECTING THE MIND

Bay or Laurel

Whether chewed, smoked, or inhaled, the Bay reputedly produced frenzy, hallucinations, and visions, as exemplified by the Pythia, the priestess of the Delphic Oracle, who fell into a prophetic trance and prophesied. On the other hand, it is an established fact the Bay leaves are non-toxic, so the question remains – what did the Pythia chew? It has been suggested there were toxic fumes emanating from the clefts in the rocks over which the Pythia sat, which induced her trance.

Fly Agaric

The juice of the Fly Agaric mushroom causes hallucinations, transcendental states, and intoxication. The followers of Dionysus and his priests did chew the mushroom, which would explain the characteristic wild behaviour of the Maenads.

The 'ambrosia', the food of the gods, allegedly contained the juice of the mushroom, hence the agaric was regarded as sacred.

Lotos

The Lotos (or Zizyphus) tree is named after a nymph called Lotis. She attracted amorous attentions of Priapus, a very ugly god with huge genitals. As he pursued her, she, not surprisingly, tried to get away from him, calling out to all gods for help. They answered her prayers by changing her in the nick of time into a Lotos tree.

The tree retained great powers of transformation. It happened to Dryope, daughter of the king of Oechalia while she and her sister Iole sat under it, playing with her infant son. Suspecting nothing she plucked the fruit of the tree for the baby to play with, only to be instantly transformed into a Lotos tree.

There is a detailed description of the eaters of the Lotos fruit in the Odyssey. They were members of a tribe living on the Libyan coast and on the island of Menynx called also Lotophagitis after the Lotos trees growing there. The tranquilising effect of the fruit made them pass the time in languid daydreaming, undisturbed by worries and responsibilities.

Sailing home to Ithaca, Odysseus and his crew found themselves in the land of the Lotos Eaters when blown off course as they rounded Cap Malea. The fruit affected the crew in the same way, making them languid and oblivious to the outside world. Odysseus became worried he would have no one to man the sails if they extended their stay and had to drag away his companions by force.

Theophrastus made a thorough study of the tree and its fruit. He described the fruit – it was the size of a pea, had no kernel, it changed colour as it ripened just like the grapes, and had a sweet, pleasant taste. It was also quite harmless and produced none of the properties described by Homer. Whole armies fed on it without any side effects, and indeed it was considered wholesome, providing immunity to stomach upsets.

The Lotos tree is still grown and cultivated for its fruit, its curious drug-like qualities described by Homer are an unsolved mystery.

Lupin

It was believed that Lupins help brighten the mind and imagination. Protogenes, the celebrated painter of Rhodes, reputedly lived on Lupins and water while painting.

ADDITIONAL NOTES

Anise – Pimpinella anisum

Sprigs on the body prevented bad dreams.

Poison nut- Strychnos nux-vomica

Theophrastus: 'This plant can drive a person mad.'

Poppy – Papaver somniferum

Yields mind-altering opium.

REMEMBRANCE AND THE AFTERLIFE

The Underworld

The ruler of the underworld where all 'who have done away with life'[213] descended, was Zeus's brother, Hades. He seldom made his appearance on earth, and wore a helmet of invisibility when he did, hence his title, 'The Unseen'. No favours were asked or expected of him, and no temples were dedicated to him. One notable exception was recorded by Pausanias. He mentioned a temple in Elis erected by the Eleans who worshipped Hades, 'the only men I know who do so'. The Eleans believed Hades had fought on their side in a struggle in the distant past and regarded him as a friendly deity. The temple was open only once a year, because men go down to Hades only once.

All the mineral riches buried in the earth belonged to him, hence his other title 'The Giver of Wealth'. On the whole he was not interested in what went on in the upper regions. On one occasion he was wounded by the arrow of Heracles, who 'shot him at the Gate of Hell among the dead and left him to his anguish'. In excruciating pain, Hades crawled to Mount Olympus where 'Peon the Healer spread soothing ointments on the wound and cured him; for after all he was not made of mortal

---

[213] Homer – *The Odyssey*

stuff'.[214]

Hades reappeared briefly when he saw Persephone, daughter of the corn goddess Demeter, picking flowers in a field, and fell in love with her. Not given to extended courtship he sent up a beautiful Narcissus to lure her. As she bent down to pick it, the earth opened at her feet, up jumped Hades in a magnificent chariot drawn by black horses, swept her up and retreated instantly to his underground kingdom. The earth closed behind them, leaving no trace. It took Persephone's mother, Demeter, a long time to discover what had happened and to recover her daughter. When she did, it was too late. By that time Persephone had tasted the food of the dead, which committed her forever to the underworld. It was only thanks to Zeus's intercession that Demeter managed to force Hades to a compromise, which allowed Persephone to spend part of the year with her in the upper regions.

Once with Hades in the underworld, no longer the cherished Maiden ('Kore'), daughter of Demeter, but the Queen of the Dead, she:

Waits for all men born,
Forgets the earth her mother
The life of fruit and corn,
And spring and seed and swallow
Take wing for her and follow
Where summer song rings hollow
And flowers are put to scorn.[215]

Unlike the other Olympian deities, Hades and Persephone led an uneventful, childless existence, rarely attracting attention. There were just two occasions of Hades' infidelity. Once a nymph called Menthe caught his fancy. Persephone stepped in, changing Menthe into a Mint plant, reputedly to trample her underfoot. Hades had one more try, this

---

[214] Homer, *Iliad, V*, Penguin 1972, tr. E. V. Rieu, p.102-103
[215] A. C. Swinburne *The Garden of Proserpine*

time with a nymph called Leuce, only to see her transformed into a White Poplar tree. This stands by the pool of Memory in the fields of Asphodel in the bloomless garden of Persephone. The fields of Asphodel were the designated place of eternal rest for the majority of 'the unheeding dead, the phantoms of men outworn'. Homer referred to it often. Achilles, for instance, 'whose feet had been so fleet on earth passed with great strides down the meadows of asphodel', or 'the giant hunter Orion who was rounding up the game on the meadows of asphodel'[216].

Why, one might ask, of all plants, did the choice fall on the Asphodel? It had been suggested that it was for its lack of appealing qualities. A plant incapable of giving pleasure matched the vision of the infinitely dull greyness of the underworld, in other words, an uninspiring plant for undistinguished lives, or lives not distinguished enough to feast with the gods. To others, however, the pointed, spear-shaped inflorescences suggested the image of a regiment of ghosts marching on the shores of Acheron, one of the rivers of the underworld.

The Asphodel was often planted on graves as a symbol of mourning, possibly also as a symbolic provision of food for the journey to the other world. Asphodel tubers, rich in starch, were a source of food in times of famine, though some people managed to thrive on it. Epimenides, one of the seven sages of Athens, reputedly existed on a diet of Asphodel and water for fifty years.

The subterranean world of the dead was accessible by various holes and clefts in the ground, or by caves. The traffic was one way only; once entered, never left. The exit was permanently guarded by a monstrous dog – Cerberus. It came up to the upper region only once, much against its will, dragged up by Heracles in one of his twelve Labours. As they struggled, from its spittle sprang the Aconites, while the sweat from

---

[216] Homer *The Odyssey, XI,* 538-540, *A Gathering of Shades*, tr. E. V. Rieu, Alan Lane 1973, pp.185,186

Heracles' brow bleached the underside of the leaves of the Poplar wreath he wore at the time.

It was a gloomy place. When Odysseus met the soul of Achilles during the Gathering of Shades and complimented him on how lucky he was to be 'a mighty prince among the dead', Achilles answered him scornfully: 'Spare me your praise of death. Put me on earth again and I would rather be a serf in the house of some landless man with little enough for himself to live on, than king of all these dead men that have done with life'[217]. Those were the words of a hero, who died a hero's death, the highest aspiration of every Greek. What then could an ordinary man expect to await him in the afterlife?

In order to reach the eternal place of rest, the soul of the deceased had to cross the river Styx, 'the dark and terrible oath-stream of the gods.'[218] (The oath taken by gods as they drank its waters remained unbroken, on pain of dire punishment).

For the crossing it had to pay the ferryman, a dour miser called Charon. Those who received proper burial rites had a small coin (an obol) placed under the tongue for this purpose. Woe to those who had no coin to pay him – they were doomed to wander for ever on the deserted shore.

Such then were the prospects the Greeks believed awaited the majority of people after death. While most souls went to the fields of Asphodel, the wicked were taken to a place of punishment, to the depths of Tartarus. For the select few, the heroes and the virtuous, were reserved the Elysian Fields and the Isles of the Blessed:

For them the sun shines at full strength – while we here walk in the night.
The plains around their city are red with roses,
and shaded by incense trees heavy with golden fruit.

---

[217] *The Odyssey XI*, tr. E. V. Rieu, Alan Lane 1973, p.184
[218] IRF 2,858, p.123

And some enjoy horses and wrestling, or table games and the lyre
and near them blossoms a flower of perfect joy.
Perfumes always hover above the land
from the frankincense strewn in deep-shining fire of the god's altars.
And across from them the sluggish rivers of black night
Vomit forth a boundless gloom.[219]

This was beyond the expectations of the majority. They accepted death with resignation, a price to be paid for life, yet preferable to life without honour.

... but of us who must die
why should a man sit in darkness
and cherish to no end
an old age without a name ...

asks Pindar[220].

Immortality essentially meant living in human memory, hence the heroic deeds, the striving for excellence and glory in order to leave a lasting impression on future generations. The highest honour the gods could bestow on a mortal was to set his name among the stars, emblazoned across the sky for all to see, or transform him into a plant to be remembered in everyday life.

THE PLANTS OF THE AFTERLIFE

The evergreen plants, their colour unchanging with the fluctuations of the seasons, were symbolic of immortality. Other commendable characteristics were resistance to decay and durability, denotative of

---

[219] Pindar: *The Elysian Fields* tr. Willis Barnstone, p.105, *Greek Literature in Translation*, Penguin
[220] Pindar, *The Odes, Olympian 1*, 83-84, tr. C. M. Bowra, p.67

perpetuity, the 'being forever in one's memory'. A fine example is the splendid Cedar which also represented strength, grandeur, and, thanks to the decay-resistant quality of its wood, incorruptibility, symbolic of immortality.

Pine

The evergreen Pine signified immortality, its resin incorruptibility. The reason for worshipping it and its association with immortality is best explained by James Frazer:[221] 'Perhaps the sight of its changeless, though sombre green, cresting the ridges of the high hills above the fading splendour of the autumn woods in the valleys may have seemed to their eyes to mark it out as the seat of a diviner life, of something exempt from the vicissitudes of the seasons, constant and eternal as the sky which stooped to meet it'.

Parsley

The popular culinary herb, Parsley was symbolic of mourning. It was commonly strewn over graves and garlanded corpses, so that the saying 'to be in need of parsley' came to imply that a person was about to die.

At the Nemean games, athletes competed for a wreath of Parsley in memory of the disasters of the Peloponnesian wars. Its symbolism goes back to the time of the 'Seven against Thebes'. (The Seven were to lead an army against the city of Thebes. All lost their lives). Action was preceded by an incident involving the infant son of Lycurgus King of Nemea, Archemorus, who was put on a bed of Parsley by his nurse, and was killed by a lurking viper. It was interpreted as an omen of disaster for the seven chieftains who were at that time visiting Nemea, and the child was called the 'Forerunner of Death'. To commemorate this event the Nemean games were established.

On the other hand, Wild Parsley woven into wreaths and chaplets,

---

[221] J. G. Frazer *The Golden Bough*

was commonly worn at banquets in the belief it created gaiety and increased appetite. Together with Rue it was believed to ward off evil spirits.

Black Poplar

The Black Poplar, symbol of the autumn equinox, was a tree of sorrow, lost hope and dying. A grove of Black Poplars and Willows surrounding the entrance to the underworld was described by Circe when she told Odysseus the way to 'steer [to] Persephone's deserted strand and grove/dusky with poplars and the drooping willow'[222]. Unfortunately, the present-day visitor shown the entrance to the Tartarus on the southernmost tip of the Peloponnese, will find the grove no longer there. Theophrastus mentioned a Black Poplar growing by the entrance to a cave on Mount Ida, where it was customary to hang dedicatory offerings.

According to legend the Heliades, sisters of the sun-hero Phaeton, were transformed into Poplars to enable them to weep for ever over the loss of their brother as he crashed the sun chariot. Every morning their father, the sun-god Helios, drove the sun in a four-horse chariot across the sky. Phaeton kept begging to let him have a go, until Helios finally, albeit reluctantly, agreed. (The horses, by the way, were fed on herbs from the islands of the Blessed). Phaeton soon lost control. As the chariot careered across the sky, the sun rolled up and down, either scorching the earth or freezing it. This drew Zeus's attention. Vexed with the youngster, he killed him with a thunderbolt. Phaeton fell into the river Eridanus (present-day Po). His sisters, the Heliades, who allegedly harnessed the horses, came down to mourn him. They were transformed into Black Poplars, forever weeping tears of amber into the river.

Above the waters of Eridanos

---

[222] OFTZ 10, p.192

Where, in lament for Phaethon,
His sisters drop their piteous tears
Which glow like amber in the dark stream."[223]

Fact and fiction are not far apart in ancient legends. The river Po marked the southern end of the Northern trade route for the much-valued amber. Recent archaeological excavations of the area have brought to light a large hoard of amber buried near the river. Amber, extremely rare and precious, was used in ornamentation and in jewellery. Penelope, the wife of Odysseus, for instance, was given 'a necklace wrought in gold, with sunray pieces of clear, glittering amber'[224] by one of her suitors.

PLANTS DEDICATED TO THE DEITIES OF THE UNDERWORLD

Cypress

To Hades belonged the decay-resistant Cypress, ever regarded as the tree of sorrow, mourning, and death. It was said the Cypress, once cut down, will never spring up from its roots. A Cypress branch hung outside the house where a death had taken place, informed of the event. The Cypress wood, because of its resistance to decay, was often used for coffins.

It was believed that the spirits of the deceased liked to wander among the Cypress groves dedicated to their memory. Cypresses were also commonly planted in places of burial, a practice persisting to the present day, lining the walls of village cemeteries.

According to legend, the Cypress tree owes its origin to a youth, beloved of Apollo, called Cyparissus, who accidentally killed his favourite stag. Overcome with sorrow and remorse, he wept and wept

---

[223] Euripides *Hippolytus*, tr. Philip Vellacot, Penguin 1974, p.105
[224] *The Odyssey*, Book 15,

and would not be consoled. Finally, Apollo took pity on him and changed him into a cypress tree so that he could mourn the loss of his stag for ever.

Maidenhair fern

The Maidenhair Fern was sacred both to Hades and Persephone. It was thought to possess the property of repelling water, because of the way water droplets collect on its leaves. Theophrastus noticed that water would not stay on them and described the Fern as 'wet-proof'. Water is symbolic of life, as numerous references to 'water of life', 'spring of living water' etc. testify. Conversely, lack of water implied loss of life and extinction, hence its association with the rulers of the kingdom of the dead.

Yew

The sombre, slow-growing Yew with its red berries, the colour of the food of the dead, was sacred to Hecate, the powerful goddess of magic and witches. It is associated with death and cemeteries to this day.

Willow

The Willow, symbolic of grief and death, was the tree of the death goddesses – the triple-headed goddess Hecate, Persephone, and the witch goddess Circe. It grew together with the Black Poplar in the so-called Grove of Persephone, which surrounded the entrance to the underworld.

Circe also had Willows growing in her grove in Colchis – not a true grove, rather a cemetery by which Jason and the Argonauts passed on their way to fetch the Golden Fleece. There they saw male corpses wrapped in untanned ox hides hanging from the tops of the Willow trees. The extent of their horror can only be surmised, as proper burial rites were held sacred, and nothing could have been more shocking than their violation.

Persephone had a sacred wood in Phokis where grew Poplars and Willows.

Juniper

The prickly Juniper was dedicated to the terrible deities of the underworld – the Erinnyes or Furies, spirits of Vengeance. They sprang from blood trickling from the wound of Uranus,[225] castrated by Cronus. The Furies, who punished men for broken oaths, never released their victims and would chase them beyond the ends of the earth, even to the underworld. The rough, thorny Juniper is not a surprising choice for those spiteful deities. Its root, burned as incense, was believed to be the most acceptable to them. On the other hand, burning its berries reputedly banished evil influences.

The object of the expedition of the Argonauts to Colchis (Asia Minor) was to fetch the Golden Fleece. It hung in a grove on an Oak tree guarded by a dragon that never slept. They were only able to secure it thanks to the sorceress Medea, who took a freshly cut Juniper branch, sacred to the chthonic deities, dipped it in a magic potion, and sprinkled it into the eyes of the dragon, instantly sending it to sleep.[226]

Poppy

The sleep-inducing properties of the Poppy were already recognised in antiquity. It was dedicated to the twin divinities, Hypnos (sleep) and Thanatos (death), as well as to Morpheus (dreams). The drug 'morphine' extracted from the gum is named after him.

The red colour of the Poppy recommended it as the symbol of oblivion and death. A possible reason might be traced to the Odyssey. When Odysseus met the dead souls at the place pointed to him by the goddess Circe, the shades were only able to communicate with him once they had drunk of the sacrificial blood. The red colour of the blood may have given rise to the belief that it was the colour of the food of the dead. It was

---

[225] Pre-classical deity Uranus was husband of Ge (Earth), father of the Titans. Cronus was the youngest of the Titans.
[226] C. Kerenyi *The Heroes of the Greeks*, pub. Thames & Hudson, 1997, p. 266

further confirmed by Persephone who, while fretting in the underworld after her abduction, ate seven seeds of the pomegranate (whose flesh is red). Pigs sacred to the death goddesses were fed on red cornelian cherries. Red beans were believed to house the souls of the dead.

Poppies, together with ears of corn, were offered to Demeter whose cult was joined with her daughter's, Persephone, the Queen of the Dead.

BURIALS AND FUNERALS

The Greek funerary art concentrated on the theme of departure without tears, lamentations, or exaggerated expressions of grief. Representations on funerary *stelae* might show a woman putting away her jewels getting ready for a long journey, mourners gathering round a funerary meal, a limp warrior carried by the winged deities Sleep or Death, their very restraint creating a haunting impression of profound sadness.

Correct performance and fulfilment of burial rites were paramount. Not to do so was not only unthinkable, it was an outrage, subject to civic punishment. This is the theme of the play *Antigone* by Sophocles, where the heroine Antigone was determined to bury with honours her dead brother fallen in a battle, in contravention of the decree of the city's tyrant Creon, who was just as determined to refuse them.

In the story of the Argonauts and The Golden Fleece, Medea and Jason were able to get away from the pursuing ship, which slowed down to pick up the pieces of her brother's body to give him a proper burial.

In the Odyssey, at the Gathering of the Dead Souls, the first to meet Odysseus was a member of his crew, fatally wounded in a fall from a roof, and left unburied. 'I beseech you my prince,' he cries, 'do not leave me unburied and unwept ... Bury me with all my arms such as they are, and raise a mound for me on the shore'.[227]

The obligatory coin, the obol, placed under the tongue of the deceased to pay the ferryman Charon, was part of the ritual. There were no consistent burial customs concerning the disposal of the body. At one stage bodies were burned on pyres and their ashes put into urns. Uncremated bodies were placed in coffins. The dead were separated from the living by being deposited in cemeteries outside the city gates early on in history. In Athens only the bodies of heroes could be buried within the limits of the city.

Burial plots outside the city became veritable little gardens dedicated to the memory of the dead, planted with flowers and bushes, lovingly tended, often provided with watering wells and even dining pavilions for family meals to be consumed on the anniversary of the deceased's death. The participants wore wreaths, songs of praises were sung, libations of wine and milk were poured. Fruit and cakes were placed in special containers with holes at the bottom, so that the contents could drain down to the deceased.[228] Their representations (either a painting or a sculpture) were placed in the house and crowned twice a month with laurel.

Mint

The herb Mint owes its appearance to the transformation of the unfortunate nymph Menthe (or Minthe) who happened to catch Hades' eye, by his jealous wife, Persephone, so that she could trample her underfoot. Its sharp smell recommended it for use in funerals.

Iris

This flower is named after the goddess Iris, the messenger of the goddess Hera, who guided the souls of women to their place of rest. Through

---

[227] *The Odyssey XI*, tr. E. V. Rieu, Book Club Ass.1973 p.173
[228] RFG p.196

association with her it was planted on women's graves.

The 'Mourning Iris' came into being at the transformation of the maiden companions of Persephone Queen of the Dead, who followed her into the underworld.

Narcissus

The lovely Narcissus, chosen by Hades to lure Persephone to a place where he could abduct her and carry her off to his kingdom, became associated with the underworld. The mortals offered it to its dreadful inhabitants the Furies (or Erinnyes) lurking there. It was planted on graves and woven into funerary wreaths.

Myrtle

This evergreen shrub, principally sacred to Aphrodite the goddess of love, was also associated with grief and death, and commonly strewn on graves. Apparently, it lined the paths in the underworld where the disconsolate walked. Dionysus bribed Persephone with a gift of Myrtle to release his mother, Semele, from the underworld.

Myrtle wreaths were much in evidence in funeral rites adorning the dead, their gravestones, and the relatives of the deceased. In Athens the bodies of the fallen in battle were brought to the city, where the bereaved wearing wreaths of Myrtle, brought fresh branches decorated with woollen ribbons offerings together with garlands and wreaths of flowers. In the rites conducted privately, a wreath of flowers was put on the head of the deceased laid out on a bier before burial. Later, a statuette of the deceased standing by the domestic altar was crowned with a Myrtle wreath twice a month, and on the seventh day of the new moon.[229]

The inhabitants of Thebes held funeral games in commemoration of the children of Heracles, killed by him in a fit of madness sent by Hera. The winner received a wreath of Myrtle.

---

[229] RFG, p. 197

ADDITIONAL NOTES

PLANTS OF MOURNING

Basil- *Ocimum basilicum*

A herb of grief and death, also capable of averting bad luck.

Hyssop – *Hyssopus officinalis*

Used in funeral purification rites. The house where death took place was purified with sea water and hyssop.[230]

Beans – *Phaseolus vulgaris*

Believed to house the souls of the dead (particularly the red variety). To eat them was paramount to eating one's parents' heads, according to Orpheus, founder of the mystic cult of Orphism.

Rosemary – *Rosmarinus officinalis*

A herb of remembrance

Laurel – *Laurus nobilis*

Crowned members of the family of the deceased on the celebrations of their anniversaries.

Box – *Buxus sempervirens*

Like all evergreen plants, Box was a symbol of immortality and burial, sacred to Hades, ruler of the underworld, and Cybele the Phrygian Mother of the Gods.

---

[230] RFG p.82

Ivy – Hedera helix

Association with the god Dionysus apart, the evergreen, tenacious Ivy, symbolic of the cycle of death and rebirth, was linked also to Attis, lover of Cybele.

SCIENTIFIC NAMES OF PLANTS
MENTIONED IN THE CHAPTERS

FLOWERS

Anemone	*Anemone coronaria*
Bears' Breech	*Acanthus mollis*
Coltsfoot	*Tussilago farfara*
	Gladiolus communis (Sword Lily – *Gladiolus italicus*)
Giant Fennel	*Ferula communis*
Honesty	*Lunaria annua*
Hyacinth	*Hyacinthus orientalis*
Larkspur	*Consolida regalis*
Narcissus	*Narcissus poeticus*
Pheasant's Eye	*Adonis annua*
Squill	*Urginea maritima*

WREATHS

Bay	*Laurus nobilis*
Dill	*Anethum graveolens*
Ivy	*Hedera helix*
Lotus	*Lotus cytisoides and L.edulis*

Myrtle	*Myrtus communis*
Oak	*Quercus spp.*
Palm	*Arecaceae spp. (*Date palm – *Phoenix dactylifera)*
Parsley	*Petroselinum crispum*
Pine	*Pinus spp.*
Wild Olive	*Olea europaea spp.sylvestris*

SCENTS

Aloe	*Aloe vera*
Cedar	*Cedrus libani*
Cinnamon	*Cinnamomum zeylanicum*
Coco grass	*Cyperus rotundus*
Coco grass	*Cyperus rotundus* (or Nut Grass)
Galbanum	*Ferula gummosa*
Gilliflower	*Matthiola incana* (or Stock)
Henna	*Lawsonia inermis*
Iris	*Iris unguicularis and I.lutescens*
Jasmine	*Jasminum officinale*
Laudanum	*Cistus ladaniferus*
Lily	*Lilium candidum*
Quince	*Cydonia vulgaris*
Rose	*Rosa damascena and R.centifolia*
Saffron Crocus	*Crocus sativus*
Spikenard	*Nardostachys jatamansi* (or Nard)
Storax	*Styrax officinalis*
Sweet Acacia	*Acacia arabia and A.albida*
Syrian Balanos	*Balanites aegyptiaca*
Terebinth	*Pistacia terebinthus*
Violet	*Viola spp.*

INCENSE

| Balsam of Mecca | *Commiphora opobalsamum* |

Bay	*Laurus nobilis*
Cinnamon	*Cinnamomum zeylanicum*
Frankincense	*Boswellia sacra*
Galbanum	*Ferula gummosa*
Laudanum	*Cistus ladaniferus*
Myrrh	*Commiphora myrrha*
Verbena	*Verbena officinalis*

MUSIC

Reed (Giant)	*Arundo donax*

SPINNING, BASKETS

Flax	*Linum usitatissimum*; Wild flax – *L. bienne*
Willow	*Salix spp.*

TREES

Ash	*Fraxinus excelsior*
Black poplar	*Populus nigra*
Cedar	*Cedrus libani*
Cypress	*Cupressus sempervirens*
Ebony	*Diospyros ebenum.*
Elm	*Ulmus glabra* (Wych elm)
Fig	*Ficus carica*
Hazel	*Corylus avellana*
Lime (or Linden)	*Tillia europaea*
Oak	*Quercus spp.*
Olive	*Olea europaea*
Palm	*Arecaceae spp.* Date palm – *Phoenix dactylifera*
Pine	*Pinus spp.*
Plane	*Platanus orientalis*
White Poplar	*Populus alba*
Wild olive	*Olea europaea spp.sylvestris*

| Willow | *Salix spp.* |

SHRUBS

Cornelian cherry	*Cornus mas*
Laurel/Bay	*Laurus nobilis*
Mastic	*Pistacia lentiscus*
Myrtle	*Myrtus communis*

CEREALS

Barley	*Hordeum vulgare & H.distichon*
Chaste Tree	*Vitex agnus-castus*
Pomegranate	*Punica granatum*
Rye	*Secale cereale*
Wheat	*Triticum spp.*

SPICES

Angelica	*Angelica archangelica*
Anise	*Pimpinella anisum*
Balm	*Melissa officinalis*
Basil	*Ocimum basilicum*
Bay	*Laurus nobilis*
Borage	*Borago officinalis*
Celery	*Apium graveolens*
Cinnamon	*Cinnamomum zeylanicum*
Coriander	*Coriandrum sativum*
Cumin	*Cuminum cyminum*
Dill	*Anethum graveolens*
Elecampane	*Inula helenium*
Fennel	*Foeniculum vulgare*
Ginger	*Zingiber officinale*
Horseradish	*Armoracia rusticana*
Juniper	*Juniperus communis*

Liquorice	*Glycyrrhiza glabra*
Marjoram	*Origanum spp.*
Mustard	*Sinapsis arvensis* (Wild mustard)
Pennyroyal	*Mentha pulegium*
Pepper	*Piper nigrum*
Poppy	*Papaver rhoeas,* Opium poppy - *P.somniferum*
Rosemary	*Rosmarinus officinalis*
Rue	*Ruta graveolens*
Saffron crocus	*Crocus sativus*
Sage	*Salvia officinalis*
Savoury	*Satureja montana* (Satureja)
Sesame	*Sesamum indicum*
Southernwood	*Artemisia abrotanum* (or Lad's Love)
Sweet Cecily	*Myrrhis odorata*
Sweet Woodruff	*Galium odoratum*
Tarragon	*Artemisia dracunculus*
Thyme	*Thymus vulgaris and T.capitatus*
Wormwood	*Artemisia absinthium*

VEGETABLES

Bean	*Phaseolus spp.*
Cabbage	*Brassica oleracea*
Celery	*Apium graveolens var.dulce*
Cucumber	*Cucumis sativus*
Garlic, onion, leek	*Allium spp.*
Lentil	*Lens culinaris*
Mallow	*Malva sylvestris*
Parsley	*Petroselinum crispum*
Rue	*Ruta graveolens*
Silphium	*Ferula narthex or Ferula foetida*

ROOTS AND POT HERBS

Asparagus	*Asparagus officinalis*

Asphodel	*Asphodelus spp.*
Beet	*Beta vulgaris*
Corn Flag	*Gladiolus segetum* (Wild gladiolus is *G.italicus)*
Dodder	*Cuscuta europaea*
Globe artichoke	*Cynara scolymus (Cardoon – C.cardunculus)*
Hyssop	*Hyssopus officinalis*
Pea	*Pisum sativum*
Raddish	*Raphanus sativus*
Salsify	*Tragopogon porrifolius*
Tassel Hyacinth	*Muscari comosum*
Turnip	*Brassica rapa*

SALAD PLANTS

Chervil	*Anthriscus carefolium*
Chives	*Allium schoenoprasum*
Lettuce	*Lactuca sativa*
Lovage	*Levisticum officinale*
Nettle	*Urtica dioica*
Rocket	*Eruca sativa*
Samphire	*Crithmum maritimum*

FRUIT

Apple	*Malus domestica*
Bitter Almond	*Prunus dulcis var.amara*
Cherry	*Prunus avium* and *P.cerasus*
Citron	*Citrus medica*
Common jujube	*Zizyphus jujuba*
Date Palm	*Phoenix dactylifera*
Fig	*Ficus carica*
Grapes	*Vitis vinifera*
Pear	*Pyrus communis*
Pomegranate	*Punica granantum*
Quince	*Cydonia vulgaris*

Strawberry tree	*Arbutus unedo*
Sweet Almond	*Prunus dulcis var.dulcis*
Walnut	*Juglans regia*

MEDICINAL PLANTS

Agrimony	*Agrimonia eupatoria*
All heal	*Prunella vulgaris* (or Self heal)
Aloe	*Aloe vera*
Asphodel	*Asphodelus spp.*
Balm Lemon	*Melissa officinalis*
Bear's Breech	*Acanthus mollis*
Belladonna	*Atropa belladonna*
Betony	*Stachys officinalis*
Birthwort	*Aristolochia clematitis*
Bistort	*Bistorta officinalis*
Bitter Vetch	*Vicia orobus*
Bitumen Pea	*Psoralea bituminosa* (The Arabian Pea)
Black hellebore	*Veratrum nigrum*
Bramble	*Rubus fruticosus* (or Blackberry)
Bugloss	*Echium creticum*
Carrot	*Daucus carota*
Centaury	*Centaurium erythraea*
Chamomile Roman	*Anthemis nobilis*
Chaste Tree	*Vitex agnus-castus*
Clover	*Trifolium spp.*
Cuckoo Pint	*Arum maculatum*
Coriander	*Coriandrum sativum*
Corn Cockle	*Agrostemma githago*
Cress	*Lepidium sativum*
Cyclamen	*Cyclamen hederifolium* (or Sowbread)
Dandelion	*Taraxacum officinale*
Dittany	*Origanum dictamnus*
Elecampane	*Inula helenium*
Eryngo	*Eryngium creticum*

Fennel	*Foeniculum vulgare*
	Tanacetum parthenium (syn. with *Chrysanthemum parthenium*)
Fig	*Ficus carica.*
Flax	*Linum usitatissimum*
Gentian	*Gentiana lutea*
Germander	*Teucrium polium*
Globularia	*Globularia alypum*
Gold Flower	*Chrysanthemum segetum*
Ground ivy	*Glechoma hederacea*
Hawthorn	*Crataegus oxycantha & C.laevigata*
Helleborine	*Veratrum album* (White False Hellebore)
Henbane	*Hyoscyamus niger & H.aureus.*
Hog's Fennel	*Peucedanum officinale*
Juniper	*Juniperus communis*
Lady's Mantle	*Alchemilla filicaulis*
Larkspur	*Consolida ajacis* (Giant larkspur)
Lavender	*Lavandula spp.*
Leek	*Allium ampeloprasum var. porrum*
Lentil	*Lens culinaris*
Leontice	*Leontice leontopetalum*
Leopard's bane	*Doronicum caucasicum*
Male fern	*Dryopteris filix-mas*
Mallow	*Malva sylvestris*
Mandrake	*Mandragora officinarum*
Manna Ash	*Fraxinus ornus*
Marigold	*Calendula arvensis*
Marjoram	*Origanum spp.*
Marsh Mallow	*Althaea officinalis*
Mastic	*Pistacia lenticus*
Milkweed	*Asclepias spp. (sub.fam.Asclepiadoideae*
Mint	*Mentha spp.*
Mistletoe	*Viscum album*
Mugwort	*Artemisia vulgaris*
Mullein	*Verbascum thapsus*

Myrrh	*Commiphora myrrha*
Narcissus	*Narcissus poeticus*
Nettle Roman	*Urtica pilulifera*
Oleander	*Nerium oleander*
Onion & Garlic	*Allium family*
Opium poppy	*Papaver somniferum*
Opopanax	*Opopanax chironium fam. Apiaceae*
Oregano Cretan	*Origanum dictamnus*
Parsley	*Petroselinum crispum*
Plantain	*Plantago major and P.lanceolata*
Pomegranate	*Punica granatum*
Poplar black	*Populus nigra*
Purple Loosestrife	*Lythrum salicaria*
Roman nettle	*Urtica pilulifera*
Rosemary	*Rosmarinus officinalis*
Rue	*Ruta graveolens*
Sage	*Salvia officinalis*
Sea daffodil	*Pancratium maritimum*
Silphium	*Ferula spp.*
Southernwood	*Artemisia abrotanum* (Lad's love)
Spurge	*Euphorbia spp.*
Squirting cucumber	*Ecballium elaterium*
St John's-wort	*Hypericum hirsuitum*
Tansy	*Tanacetum vulgare*
Tassel Hyacinth	*Muscari comosum*
Thyme	*Thymus vulgaris*
Vervain	*Verbena officinalis* (or Verbena)
White hellebore	*Veratrum album*
Wormwood	*Artemisia absinthium*
Yarrow	*Achillea millefolium*
Yellow water lily	*Nuphar lutea*

APHRODISIACS AND CONTRACEPTIVES

Asparagus	*Asparagus officinalis*

Carrot	*Daucus carota*
Cedar	*Cedrus libani.*
Chaste Tree	*Vitex agnus-castus*
Cress	*Lepidum sativum*
Cyclamen	*Cyclamen hederifolium*
Dragon Arum	*Dracunculus vulgaris*
Enchanter's-n.shade	*Circaea lutetiana* (Enchanter's-nightshade)
Gladiolus	*Gladiolus illyricus*
Hemlock	*Conium maculatum*
Mandrake	*Mandragora officinarum*
Orchids	*Orchidaceae spp.*
Parsley	*Petroselinum crispum*
Pepper	*Piper nigrum*
Rocket	*Eruca sativa*

MAGIC, CHARMS, DRUGS, POISONS

Ash	*Fraxinus excelsior*
Bay	*Laurus nobilis*
Buckthorn	*Rhamnus alaternus*
Cinnamon	*Cinnamomum cassia* (or Cassia)
Citron	*Citrus medica*
Cowbane	*Cicuta virosa*
Crowfoot	*Ranunculus flammula*
Crown Daisy	*Chrysanthemum coronarium*
Death Cap	*Amanita phalloides*
Fly Agaric	*Amanita muscaria*
Gold Flower	*Chrysanthemum segetum*
Golden Thistle	*Scolymus hispanicus* (or Spanish Oyster Plant)
Hazel	*Corylus avellana*
Hellebore	*Helleborus lividus*
Hemlock	*Conium maculatum*
Lotos	*Ziziphus lotus (or Lotos)*
Lupin	*Lupinus spp.*

Meadow Saffron	*Colchicum autumnale*
Mistletoe	*Viscum album*
Monkshood	*Aconitum napellus and A.vulparia*
Mugwort	*Artemisia vulgaris*
Peony	*Paeonia officinalis*
Rue	*Ruta graveolens & R. chalapensis*
Smilax	*Smilax aspera*
Squill	*Urginea maritime*
Thorn Apple	*Datura stramonium*
Vervain	*Verbena officinalis*
Willow	*Salix spp.*
Wolf's Bane	*Aconitum anthora*

REMEMBRANCE AND AFTERLIFE

Asphodel	*Asphodelus fistulosus and spp.*
Cypress	*Cupressus sempervirens*
Iris	*Iris florentina*
Juniper	*Juniperus communis*
Maidenhair Fern	*Adiantum capillus-veneris*
Mint	*Mentha spp.*
Myrtle	*Myrtus communis*
Narcissus	*Narcissus poeticus*
Parsley	*Petroselinum crispum*
Pine	*Pinus spp.*
Poplar black	*Populus nigra*
Poppy	*Papaver somniferum*
Willow	*Salix spp.*
Yew	*Taxus baccata*

GLOSSARY OF GODS, FAMOUS CHARACTERS, MAIN EVENTS, AND FREQUENTLY USED NAMES AND TERMS [231]

CHARACTERS IN MYTHOLOGY, LEGEND AND LITERATURE

Gods and Immortals

God/goddess – An immortal being with powers over nature and human affairs.

The Olympian Gods – The world that emerged from **Chaos** was first ruled by **Uranus** and **Ge.** They were followed by the **Titans,** headed by **Cronus** and his wife, **Rhea.** The rebellion of their son **Zeus** led to the establishment of the **Twelve Olympian Gods**, named after their mountain home, **Olympus**, who were worshipped by the Greeks. Most of them were adopted by the Romans, who changed their names, but little else. They include **Zeus** (the ruler), **Hera, Athena, Demeter, Poseidon, Apollo, Artemis, Aphrodite, Hephaestus, Ares, Hermes, and Hestia,** replaced by **Dionysus.**

Aphrodite – goddess of love and beauty. Born of sea foam surrounding the genitals of the castrated Uranus. Occasionally called Kypris after the island of Kythera where she first landed before swimming on to Cyprus. Wife of Hephaestus, the lame smith-god. Had many lovers, mortal and immortal. Her son was **Eros**, the winged, little boy with love-smiting arrows.

---

[231] Spelling of names taken from Everyman's Classical Dictionary by John Warrington, pub. J.M.Dent & Sons ltd. 1970

Apollo – god of light, reason, law, music, healing, archery, and prophesy. His companions were the **Muses**.

Ares – god of war.

Artemis – goddess of the hunt, protector of wild animals and women, an avowed virgin, twin sister of Apollo.

Athena – goddess of war and wisdom, born from Zeus's head, patron deity of the city of Athens.

Asclepius – god of healing, son of Apollo.

Circe – goddess and sorceress on the island of Aeaea; Odysseus spent a year with her.

Cronus – a pre-Olympian deity, a Titan.

Cybele – Phrygian Great Mother of the Gods, worshipped in ecstatic rites by eunuch priests.

Demeter – goddess of corn (i.e. grain) and fruits of the earth, mother of Persephone by Zeus.

Dionysus – god of wine and good living, also patron of fruits and orchards. His female companions were the **Maenads**.

Echo – nymph in love with Narcissus.

Erinyes or **Furies** – spirits of vengeance.

Hecate – triple-bodied goddess of black magic.

Hades – god of the underworld, brother of Zeus. Abducted Persephone, daughter of Demeter, and made her his queen. She stays with him for part of the year.

Helios – sun-god, driving sun disc daily across the sky.

Hephaestus – lame smith god, husband of Aphrodite.

Hera – wife and sister of Zeus, goddess of women and marriage.

Hermes – patron deity of travellers, merchants. Also herald of Zeus and messenger of the gods. His son was the god **Pan,** half human, half goat.

Hestia – goddess of the family hearth.

Iris – goddess of the rainbow, messenger of Hera.

Muses – companions of Apollo, residing on Mount Helicon.

Nereids – sea nymphs, the fifty daughters of Nereus, the sea god.

Nymphs – beautiful girl spirits of streams, woods, mountains, and nature.

Pan – son of Hermes, Arcadian patron of flocks and shepherds.

Persephone – or **Kore** (the Maiden) daughter of Demeter, wife of Hades, queen of the underworld. Spends part of the year with her mother, part underground with Hades.

Poseidon – Zeus' brother, god of the sea and earthquakes.

Prometheus – a Titan, stole fire from the gods to give to mankind, for which he was punished by Zeus by being chained to a mountain in the Caucasus where an eagle pecked at his liver all day. It healed during the night to be pecked at again the following day. He was finally released by Heracles.

Satyrs – wild and lustful spirits with goat legs and ears, and horse tails.

Silenus – permanently drunk, lecherous Satyr, tutor to Dionysus.

Titans – pre-Olympian demi-gods.

Zeus – the greatest of Olympian gods, 'father of gods and men', god of the sky.

Heroes

Hero – a mortal or semi-mortal man or woman, who has done superhuman deeds.

Achilles – hero, second only to Heracles, the greatest of Greek warriors, famous for his exploits in the Trojan War. Defeated Hector, champion of the Trojans. Son of a mortal king of Thessaly and a sea goddess Thetis, who failed to make him immortal when holding him by the heel when immersing him in the River Styx, left it exposed to danger. Died when a poisoned arrow struck it.

Adonis – exceptionally handsome mortal lover of Aphrodite, killed by a boar.

Agamemnon – leader of the Greeks in the Trojan War, brother of Menelaus, king of Sparta and husband of Helen. Killed by his wife and her lover on his return from Troy.

Ajax – warrior and hero of Trojan War on the Greek side, second only to Achilles in bravery. Son of king of Salamis. Quarrelled with Odysseus over possession of the slain Achilles' armour. Lost the toss and went mad, slaughtering the army's sheep, mistaking them for the enemy. Committed suicide.

Argonauts – heroes led by **Jason** who sailed in the *Argo* to recover the Golden Fleece in Colchis (on the Black Sea).

Attis – young lover of **Cybele**, mother goddess of Phrygia. In remorse for having once been unfaithful to her, he castrated himself and bled to death.

Chiron – a Centaur, i.e., half-horse, half-man, referred to as 'The Wise Centaur', great healer and teacher of medicine and archery to a number of gods and heroes.

Europa – maiden, seduced by Zeus who took the form of a bull and carried her off to Crete. Mother of the kings of Crete.

Hector – hero of Trojans, son of king of Troy, killed by Achilles.

Helen – daughter of Zeus transformed into a swan by Leda, hatched from an egg. The most beautiful woman of her time, wife of Menelaus, king of Sparta, promised by the goddess Aphrodite to Paris, son of the king of Troy in the so-called 'Judgment of Paris'. Her abduction triggered the Trojan War, described in *The Iliad* by Homer. After the fall of Troy was reconciled with Menelaus and went back to Sparta. In *The*

Odyssey by Homer, she is an aging beauty living the life of domesticity. Was hanged by a grief-stricken women widowed after the Trojan War. Deified after death.

Heracles – son of Zeus by Alcmene, daughter of the king of Mycenae. The greatest hero, famed for exploits, the Twelve Labours in particular. Founder of the Olympic Games. Was inadvertently given a poisoned shirt by his wife, which seared his flesh. Unable to endure the agony he built his own funeral pyre, which no one dared to light for him until bribed with a gift. Was snatched from the burning pyre by the gods and made immortal.

Hippolytus – son of Theseus, king of Athens. His step-mother fell in love with him. When he repulsed her, she falsely accused him of assault. Theseus believed her. Incensed, he prayed to Poseidon to kill Hippolytus. Poseidon sent a sea monster to terrify the horses of Hippolytus as he was driving along a seashore. The chariot crashed against the rocks, and Hippolytus died, entangled and dragged by the reins.

Labours of Hercules performed for king Eurystheus of Argos in expiation for killing his children in a fit of madness sent by Hera:

1/slaying the Nemean lion; 2/killing of many-headed hydra of Lerna; 3/capture of the golden hind of Ceryneia; 4/bringing back alive the boar of Mount Erymanthus; 5/cleaning the Augeias' stables; 6/ getting rid of Stymphalian birds; 7/ capture of Cretan bull; 8/ bringing back the man-eating mares of king Diomedes; 9/ fetching the girdle of Hippolyte, queen of the Amazons; 10/ catching the cattle of Geryon; 11/fetching the golden apples of Hesperides; 12/ capture of the dog Cerberus of the underworld.

Maenads – frenzied companions of Dionysus.

Medea – witch, daughter of king of Colchis, priestess of Hecate.

Menelaus – king of Sparta, brother of Agamemnon, husband of Helen.

Muses – companions of Apollo.

Odysseus – principal character of *The Odyssey* by Homer, king of Ithaca, hero of the Trojan War. Husband of faithful Penelope, father of Telemachus.

Orpheus – legendary Greek musician, his music enchanted wild beasts and even trees and rocks. Married Eurydice. When she died, he charmed the gods of the underworld who gave him permission to bring her back to the upper regions, only to lose her at the last moment. Grief-stricken, singing about his lost love, was torn to pieces by jealous Thessalian women. The nightingales by his grave reputedly sing sweeter than in other places. Also founder of the mystical cult Orphism.

Paris – son of Priam, King of Troy, his abduction of Helen triggered the Trojan War.

Seven Against Thebes – brothers fighting for the rule of the city of Thebes.

Theseus – hero of Athens; killed the Minotaur, escaped the maze with help of Ariadne.

AUTHORS AND HISTORICAL/BORDERLINE CHARACTERS

Aeschylus (525-456 BC) – Athenian dramatist, author of (among others) *Prometheus Bound, Seven Against Thebes*.

Alexander the Great (356-323 BC) – king of Macedon, famed for far-reaching conquests, died in Babylon.

Dioscorides – Pedianos Dioscorides, Greek herbalist and physician in the Army of Nero (1st c. AD), author of *De Materia Medica* – an account of over six hundred medicinal plants. Quotations come from the *Herbal Englished by John Goodyear 1622-1635,* published by O.U.P. 1934 ed. Robert J. Gunther.

Euripides (480-406 BC) – Athenian dramatist, author of (among others) *Medea, The Bacchae, Hippolytus, Iphigenia in Tauris.*

Gilgamesh – ruler of the Sumerian city of Uruk, c. 2,750 BC, hero of the oldest known epic.

Herodotus (484-420 BC) – historian, 'The Father of History'. His *Histories* are mainly about the war between the Greeks and the Persians, but contain items, stories, and anecdotes about people and places where he travelled, Asia Minor and Egypt.

Hesiod – c.700 BC, poet, wrote *Works & Days* and *Theogony.*

Hippocrates (469-399 BC) – physician, 'Father of Medicine', born on the island of Cos, where he established his 'school', stressing clinical observation, recording case histories, symptoms and treatment, as well as a code of ethics embodied in the 'Hippocratic Oath'.

Homer – c.8th c. BC, to whom are attributed the epics: *The Iliad* dealing with the Trojan War and *The Odyssey* taking up the story ten years later, both masterpieces of the world's literature.

Pausanias – 2nd c. AD, traveller, author of *Guide to Greece* intended as a travel guide, now an important source of topography, history, and customs of the Greece of his day. Quotations and references come from *Guide to Greece* Vol. I & II, pub. Penguin Books 1979, translated by Peter Levi.

Pindar – Greek poet 518-438 BC, best known for *Odes* in praise of victors of athletic games.

Pliny (the Elder) – 1st c. AD Roman Scholar, author of *Natural History* (among others).

Solon (640-560 BC.) – Athenian statesman, the 'law-giver.'

Sophocles (496-406 BC) – dramatist, author of (among others) *Antigone, Oedipus The King, Electra.*

Theocritus (300-260 BC) – Greek pastoral poet, author of the *Idylls.*

Theophrastus – (370-288 BC) Greek philosopher, pupil, and successor of Aristotle. Drawn to the plant world, helped by the acquisition of Aristotle's Garden, compiled systematic and thorough observations in the *Enquiry into Plants*, hence his title 'Father of Botany'.

Thucydides (460-400 BC) – author of *The History of the Peloponnesian War*.

Xenophon (428-354 BC) – historian and general. Exiled by the Athenians for his pro-Spartan sympathies, settled in Sparta where he wrote *The Education of Cyrus*, and *Anabasis*, an account of the expedition of the ten thousand Greek mercenaries stranded in Persian territory, when the contestant to the Persian throne who hired them died.

BIBLIOGRAPHY

LIST OF BOOKS – REFERENCE AND CONSULTED

BOTANICAL

Culpeper's Complete Herbal – pub. Wordsworth 1995

Dictionary of Plants Used by Man – George Usher, pub. Constable 1974

Enquiry into Plants – Theophrastus, with English translation by Sir Arthur Hort, pub. William Heineman London/ G. P. Putnam & Sons, New York 1916

Flowers of Greece & The Aegean – A. Huxley, W. Taylor, pub. Chatto & Windus, 1977

Flora Mythologica – Dr. Johann Heinrich Dierbach, Frankfort 1833, translated into English, in M/S form (at the Kew Library)

Flowers of the Mediterranean – O. Polunin & A. Huxley, pub. Chatto & Windus, 1965

Flowering Plant Families of the World – V. H. Heywood, R. K. Brummitt, A. Culham and O. Seberg, pub. The Royal Botanic Gardens, Kew, 2007

The Garden Lore of Ancient Athens – American School of Classical Studies

The Greek Herbal of Dioscorides illustrated by a Byzantine, AD 512, translated by John Goodyear AD 1655– edited and first printed AD1933 by R. T. Gunther, pub. Oxford at University Press 1934

Guide to Medicinal Plants – Schaunberg & Ferdinand Paris, pub. Lutterworth Press, 1977

Gerard's Herbal – ed. Marcus Woodward, pub. Minerva Press, 1971

Herbals – Agnes Arber, pub. Cambridge University Press, 1912

An Illustrated History of the Herbals – F. J. Anderson, pub. Columbia University Press,1997

The Kindly Fruits – F. Bianchini and F. Corbetta, pub. Cassell, 1977

Medicinal Plants of Greece – G. Sifkas, pub. Efstathiadis Group, Athens, 1981

The Oxford Book of Food Plants – S. G. Harrison, G. M. Masefield and Michael Wallis, pub. OUP, 1969

The Power of Plants – Brendan Lehane, pub. John Murray, 1977

The Pantropheon (or History of Food and Its Preparation in Ancient Times) by Alexis Soyer, Reprint of 1853 Edition Simpkin, Marshall, London in 1853, 1997

Plant Lore, Legend and Lyrics (Embracing the Myths, Traditions, Superstitions and Folklore of the Plant Kingdom) – Richard Folkard, ed. Sampson Low, pub. Marston & Co. Ltd., London, 1892

Plants and Plant Lore in Ancient Greece – J. E. Raven, pub. Leopard's Head Press, 2000

Stearn's Dictionary of Plant Names – W. T. Stearn, pub. Cassell,1996

The Story of Plants and their Uses to Man – John Hutchinson & Ronald Melville, 1949 (?)

The Treasury of Flowers – Alice M. Coates, Phaidon Press Ltd.,1975

The Wild Flowers of Britain and N. Europe – R. Fitter, M. Blamey, pub. Collins, 1974

Wild Flowers of the Mediterranean – David Burnie, pub. Dorling Kindersley 1995

LITERATURE AND HISTORICAL

The Aeneid – Virgil, tr. Robert Fitzgerald pub. Penguin 1985

The Ancient Greeks – M. I. Finley, pub. Penguin 1963

Ancient Greeks – How They Lived and Worked – Maurice Pople pub. David & Charles, Newton Abbott, 1976

The Ancient World – T. R. Glover, pub. Penguin, 1944

Antigone – Sophocles, tr. Robert Fagles, pub. Penguin, 1988

Archaic Greece – E. Homann-Wedeking, tr. J. R. Foster, pub. Methuen, 1968

Archaeological Encyclopedia of the Holy Land – ed. Avraham Negev, pub. G. P. Putnam & Sons, New York, 1972

Ariadne's Clue – Anthony Stevens pub. Allen Lane/The Penguin Press, 1998

Art & Myth in Ancient Greece – T. H. Carpenter, pub. Thames & Hudson, 1996

Athens – Christian Meier, pub. John Murray, 1999

Attic Red Figure Vases – A survey, G. M. S. Richter, pub. Yale University Press

The Bacchae, Medea – Euripides, tr. Philip Vellacot, pub. Penguin 1972

The Bacchanals – Euripides, tr. A. S. Way, Everyman's Library, J. M. Dent & Sons London

The Song of Solomon – The Bible (King James' Version)

The Birth of Greek Art – Ekrem Akurgal tr. Wayne Dynes, pub. Methuen 1968

The Classical Greeks – Michael Grant, pub. Phoenix/Orion Books, 1989

A Companion to Greek Studies – Leonard Whibley, Cambridge University Press, 1924 and Cambridge at the University Press 1916

A Concise History of Ancient Greeks – Peter Green, pub. Book Club Ass./ Thames & Hudson, 1974

The Cyclopaedia – A. Rees, pub. 1819

Daily Life in Greece at a the time of Pericles, Robert Flacelière, tr.by Peter Green, pub. Phoenix, 2002

Dangerous Tastes, The Story of Spices – Andrew Dalby, pub. The British Museum Press, London, 2000

The Epic of Gilgamesh – tr. Andrew George pub. Penguin, 2000

The Education of Cyrus – Xenophon, tr. H. G. Dakyns, pub. J. M. Dent 1992

Folklore & Odysseys of Food and Medicinal Plants – Ernst and Joanna Lehner, pub. Farrar Straus Giroux, New York

The Glory that was Greece – J. C. Stobart pub. Sidgewick & Jackson, 1971

The Golden Ass – Apuleius, tr. Robert Graves, pub. Penguin, 1960

The Golden Bough – J. G. Frazer pub. Gramercy Books/Random House 1981

The Greek Anthology – ed. Peter Jay, pub. Allen Lane, 1973

Greek Art – John Boardman pub. Thames & Hudson, 1973

The Greek Bronze Age – Reynold Higgins, pub. The British Museum, 1970

Greek Civilization & Character – A. J. Toynbee, pub. The New American Library/A Mentor Book, 1959

The Greek Coins – Colin M. Kraay, and M. Hirmer, pub. Thames & Hudson, 1966

Greek Gods & Heroes – Ann Birchall, P. E. Corbett, pub. The British Museum, 1974

Greek Literature in Translation – ed. Michael Grant, Penguin, 1973

Greek Lyric Poetry – tr. M. L. West, pub. O.U.P., 1994

Greek Medicine – E. D. Phillips, pub. Thames & Hudson, 1973

Greek Mythology – John Pinsent pub. Hamlyn, 1969

The Greek Myths – Robert Graves pub. Penguin, 1962

Greek Painted Pottery – R. M. Cook, pub. Methuen, 1960

Greek Pastoral Poetry – tr. Anthony Holden, pub. Penguin, 1974

The Greek Philosophers – Rex Warner, A Mentor Books, The New American Library, 1963

Greek Society – Antony Andrewes, pub. Penguin, 1984

The Greek World – ed. Hugh Lloyd-Jones, pub. Penguin, 1962

The Greeks – H. D. F. Kitto – pub. Penguin, 1973

The Greeks and their Gods – W. K. C. Guthrie, pub. Methuen, 1962

The Greeks Overseas – John Boardman, Penguin, 1964

Guide to Greece Vol. I and II– Pausanias, tr. Peter Levi, pub. Penguin Books, 1979

The Handbook of Classical Mythology – Edward Tripp, pub. Arthur Baker, 1970

A Handbook of Greek Art – G. M. A. Richter, pub. Phaidon Press, 1967

The Heroes of the Greeks – C. Kerenyi pub. Thames & Hudson, 1997

Hippocrates – pub. Loeb Classical Library, 1998

Hippocratic Writings – pub. Penguin Books, 1983

An Historical Guide to the Sculpures of the Parthenon – D. E. L. Haynes, pub. The Trustees of the British Museum, 1971

Histories – Herodotus, tr. George Rawlison, pub. Wordsworth Classics 1996

The History of the Peloponnesian War – Thucydides, tr. Richard Crawley, pub. Wordsworth Classics, 1997

The Home of the Heroes – Sinclair Hood pub. Thames & Hudson, 1974

Homer and The Heroic Age – J. V. Luce, pub. Thames & Hudson, 1975

The Iliad and The Odyssey – Homer, tr. Robert Fitzgerald, pub. William Heineman, 1962 (Also tr. Robert Fagles, Penguin Classic Books 1991)

Iphigenia in Tauris; Hippolytus, Alcestis – Euripides, tr. Philip Vellacott, pub. Penguin, 1974

Landmarks in Greek Literature – C. M. Bowra, pub. Penguin, 1966

The Last Days of Socrates – Plato, tr. Hugh Tredennick, pub. Penguin, 1987

The Legacy of the Ancient World – W. G. De Burgh, pub. Penguin, 1961

The Legacy of Greece – Collection of essays ed. R. W. Livingstone, pub. Oxford at the Clarendon Press, 1924

Lysistrata, The Acharnians, The Clouds – Aristophanes, tr. Alan H. Sommerstein, pub. Penguin, 1988

The Marriage of Cadmus and Harmony – Roberto Calasso, tr. Tim Parks, pub. Vintage, 1994

Man, Nature and History – W. M. S. Russell, pub. Aldus Books, London, 1967

The Odes of Pindar, tr. C. M. Bowra, pub. Penguin, 1969

The Olympic Games – M. I. Finley and H. W. Pleket, pub. Book Club/Chatto & Windus,1967

The Oxford Book of Classical Verse in translation, ed. Adrian Poole & Jeremy Maule, pub. O.U.P.,1995

Perfume in Pictures – Margaret Woodney Wyman, Sterling Publishing Co. N.Y.,1968

The Portable Greek Historians – (Herodotus, Thucydides, Xenophon, Polybius), ed. M. I. Finley, pub. Penguin, 1982

Prehistoric Greece and Cyprus – An Archeological Handbook – Hans-

Gunter Bucch and Vassos Karageorghis, pub. Phaidon,1973

Prehistoric Religion (Study in Prehistoric Archeology) – E. O. James, pub. Thames & Hudson, 1957

Prometheus Bound, Seven Against Thebes – Aeschylus, tr. Philip Vellacott, pub. Penguin, 1988

The Rendering of Nature in early Greek Art – E. Loewy, pub.,1907

The Romance of Life in the Ancient World – F. A. Wright pub. Samson Low/Marston &Co. (undated)

Science of Mythology – C. G. Jung & C. Kerenyi pub. Ark/Routledge, 1963

Sketches from Odyssey – (unsigned booklet) pub. Athens Museum (undated)

The Survival of the Pagan Gods – Jean Seznac pub. Princeton University Press, 1972

The Uses of Greek Mythology – Ken Dowden, pub. Routledge, 2002

The Wars of Ancient Greeks – Victor Davis Hanson pub. Cassell & Co., 2000

The White Goddess – Robert Graves, pub. Faber & Faber Ltd., 1948,1974

Women in Ancient Greece – Sue Blundell, pub. The British Museum Press, 1999

Wonders of Antiquity – Leonard Cottrell, pub. Pan Books, 1964

DICTIONARIES & REFERENCES

Ariadne's Clue – Anthony Stevens, pub. Allen Lane, 1998

Classical Dictionary – John Lemprière, pub. Bracken Books, 1994

Diccionario de Simbolos (Słownik Symboli) – A. P. Chenel & A. S. Simarrof, pub. Świat Książki/Bertelsmann 2008

Dictionary of Mythology – Fernand Comte, pub. Wordsworth Classics, 1991

Dictionary of Subjects & Symbols in Art – James Hall, pub. John Murray, 1974

Dictionary of Symbolism – Hans Biederman, tr. James Hulbert, pub. Wordsworth, 1992

Dictionary of World Folklore – Alison Jones, Larousse, 1995

Everyman's Classical Dictionary – John Warrington, pub. J. M. Dent, 1970

Encyclopedia of Magic and Superstition – pub. Octopus Books, 1974

Hall's Dictionary of Subjects & Symbols in Art – pub. John Murray, 1974

An Illustrated Encyclopedia of Traditional Symbols –J. C. Cooper, pub. Thames & Hudson, 1998

Nature and its Symbols – L.I mpelluso, pub. The J. Paul Getty Museum, Los Angeles, English translation, 2004

The new Secret Language of Symbols – David Fontana, pub. Duncan Baird Publishes, 2010

New Larousse Encyclopedia of Mythology pub. Hamly 1975

      Greek Mythology – F. Guirand

      Roman Mythology – F. Guirand & A. V. Pierre

      Egyptian Mythology – F. Guirand

1000 Symbols – Rowena & Rupert Shepherd, pub. Thames & Hudson/The Ivy Press 2002

The Penguin Dictionary of Symbols – Jean Chevaliere, Alain Gheerbrant, tr. John Buchanan-Brown, pub. Penguin Books, 1996

Who's Who in the Ancient World – Betty Radice, Penguin Books, 1977

ABBREVIATIONS

IFTZ	*The Iliad* – Homer, pub. OUP 1984, tr. Robert Fitzgerald
IRF	*The Iliad* – Homer, pub. Penguin 1991, tr. Robert Fagles
OFTZ	*The Odyssey* – Homer, pub. Collins Harvill tr. Robert Fitzgerald (William Heineman 1961)
OGC	*The Odyssey* – Homer, pub. Wordsworth Classics 2002, tr. George Chapman
PGG	*Guide to Greece* – Pausanias, pub. Penguin Books 1978, tr. Peter Levi
RFG	*Daily Life in Greece at the Time of Pericles* Robert Flacelière, pub. Phoenix 2002, tr. Robert Green

ABOUT THE AUTHOR

Magdalena Czajkowska was born in Poland, settled in Britain in 1948, and has lived in London ever since. She studied Botany at Imperial College London and Art & Ancient History at the Open University. This combined interest led her to research for "The Garden of the Gods".

An established writer, she has published "The Garden of Paradise – Images of the Garden of Heaven in Art and Culture", a number of non-fiction stories and essays published in the British press, as well as translations from the Polish. Her book on the prominent Polish poet Zbigniew Herbert published in Poland was reprinted twice and adapted for the stage. Recently, she has published three books for bi-lingual children.

Made in the USA
Monee, IL
16 November 2021

82234972R00138